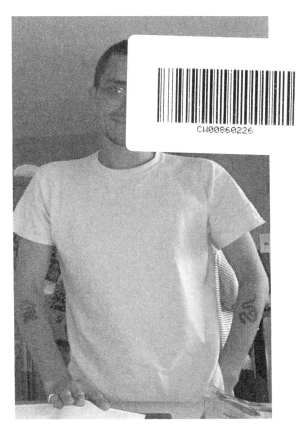

Marley's way

Why my son's not having chemo
By

Anne-Marie Hoare

Acknowledgements

Many thanks to all on Big Love for encouraging me.

To my amazingly, patient cousin, Rachel Henry for editing and proof reading. For being harsh and brutal but in the gentlest way possible.

Thank you to my other readers
Paul Thorn
Lucy Davidson
Emma Merrell
Shirley Clark
Helen Spotswood
Sarah Mila
Ruth Driver
Luciana Ferreira Day

Thanks to Simon Day for the cover design, for his patience and understanding.

Thank you to my Mum, Ruth Driver. For her encouragement and giving me the emotional toolbox to deal with this crisis and many before and since and my beautiful daughter, Annabelle for being my rock.

Big love to all the 14,000 cancer healers and carers on the Chris Wark Square One support group.

Contents

Preface

(Written in March 2018)

My son Marley was diagnosed with a malignant tumour in his chest in September 2017. Aged just 24, he was given a year to live. He underwent surgery to remove the tumour, but refused any further treatment- no chemotherapy and no radiation treatment.

This is the story of Marley's courageous decision and of his journey back to health. A story of a family experience. A cancer diagnosis effects everyone. If this book helps even one other family going through cancer, then Marley's way will not have been in vain.

We do not know what tomorrow holds for us as a family, and it is very early to start writing a story of survival. We have been told by Chris Wark (14 years cancer survivor) that two years is the magic number for healing cancer naturally, but miracle follows miracle and wonders never cease. We fully support Marley with his decision and to see him looking and feeling strong, full of vitality just four months after major surgery is wonderful. One day at a time....

One year later - March 2019

Marley passed away on 24th September 2018. Such difficult words to write not just because they are words no mother should have to write but also because after the very hesitant suggestion from my Editor, I am writing about his death at the beginning of a book that describes natural healing protocols. (Protocol: A method to be followed to control a disease.)

I have struggled so much because more than anything I do not want people to dismiss what I have written and ultimately dismiss Marley's choice by the harsh reality that he tried but didn't survive. Marley had many obstacles to overcome, a rare cancer, dissected to find an even rarer, extremely aggressive cancer (called Triton) inside.

Marley did amazingly well.

The knowledge I gained through supporting Marley and the survivors I learned about and talked to, is not something I can forget. There are thousands of cancer survivors that followed natural healing protocols living well around the world.

Do not be disheartened by his passing, but be encouraged by his story. Statistically, half of us will be diagnosed with cancer at some point in our lives. You can help prevent it. If you are diagnosed with cancer, I have seen many testimonies and survivor stories that show it can be healed with natural protocols; radically changing your diet, your lifestyle and acknowledging your emotions and exploring your spirituality. We are complex creatures and every one of these areas needs to be addressed to begin healing. These are just words on paper and the truth of the matter is it is a very difficult path to embark on but it can be done. Do not be afraid. Marley did not heal his cancer but he did heal himself in other ways and died happy with the choices he made with no regrets.

If you choose conventional treatment, then following natural protocols will lessen the side effects and you will heal quicker after surgery and radiotherapy.

So the choice is yours and that is how it should/could be for anyone with a cancer diagnosis. Whichever route someone takes sadly brings no guarantees but it's about choice and quality of life. My aim is to somehow plant a tiny seed (organic of course), for that seed to grow and spread so that maybe one-day natural protocols, good detoxing and nutritional advice will be not classed as "alternative" but a mainstay in integrative cancer treatment.

June 2019

Recently I asked a respected friend in the integrative cancer healing field to read this preface and had a long reply back, a supportive and positive reply but also a warning about The Cancer Act of 1939...I had no idea there was a Cancer Act. Yet another thing I will have to learn fast. It makes sense, as people need to be protected from bad people selling them expensive medicines or so called cures that have no scientific backing or evidence.

It also makes sense why some professionals and practitioners talked to me quite guardedly at times, and why there are lengthy disclaimers on websites. So I will have to do the same.

Disclaimer

Cancer is a too serious and complex a problem for you to deal with on your own, or simply with the help of a book, a webpage or attendance at a seminar. Go and see your doctor.

The Cancer Act 1939

An Act to make further provision for the treatment of cancer, to authorise the Minister of Health to lend money to the National Radium Trust, to prohibit certain advertisments relating to cancer, and for purposes connected to matters aforesaid.

4. **Prohibition of certain advertisements.**

(1) No person shall take part in the publication of any advertisement-

    (a)   containing an offer to treat any person for cancer, or to prescribe any remedy therefor, or to give advice in connection with the treatment thereof.

Think I can get away with saying this book is about Marley's way!
And is in no way intended to advertise any product.

A word from Marley

A wonderful gift found after his death.

Gracie, Marley's Ex and best friend, found a post Marley had written to a Neurofibromatosis type 1 Facebook group in March 2018. Finding things like this is such a lovely surprise. This is so special as Marley never really wrote of his challenge or spoke about it so openly.

"Sup, I'm Marley I'm from UK, I was diagnosed with NF1 when I was 12 following an eye test. Since then my eyesight has slowly decreased. I always had lots of birthmarks and cafe au lait spots. Last year I just graduated from a studying music production and was about to start an MA in Sonic Media.

At the start of the summer I began to fall very ill with headaches, earache, stomach ache etc. that were persistent for weeks. I got to the point were working was too much to handle as id become exhausted by midday. From there I decided that maybe things were out of my control and that I needed more help than advice from my GP. I returned home to live with my parents and booked a consultation with the doctor that diagnosed me with NF.

After a few tests I found I had a large tumour growing in my chest, I knew what the deal was but to be sure of what it was I then went through a few months of tests, biopsies and scans to find out that the tumour was malignant. I was diagnosed with a peripheral nerve sheath sarcoma. As it was growing against my Vagus nerve it explained all my symptoms.

In November I had the surgery for removal and it was all a success, despite all the complication that came before. After the post biopsy other cells had been found in the tumour belonging to a group called triton.

From a young age I had seen close friends and family all pass due to cancer and the side effects of treatment, it was mainly this that lead me to the decision to turn down all conventional treatment pre and post operation to focus on a holistic approach.

Big love to the surgeons, oncology team, nutritionists, my gym coach and all the people that believed me and supported me, as I wouldn't of been able to do what I'm doing without them.

I hope now I can return the support to help others and you. I've said quite a lot now more than I say most days. I hope everyone is having a nice day, winter doesn't seem to want to leave here yet but the sun was out the other morning so I though it was a good time for a selfie. Again I'm Marley, I'm 24 I'm from England and I have NF1".

Introduction

I asked Laura Bond (author) if I could use this title (Why my son's not having chemo) and she sent a lovely email back saying "Of course". It was important for me to use a title almost the same as hers ('My mum's not having chemo'), because even before my son was diagnosed, that is exactly what I put into Google for information and her book came up. It gave me hope and courage and I hope that any parents or carers who need the same help will be able to see Marley's story without too much searching.

Just like my son, this book is not conventional and needs some explanation.

I started this book as a diary, of sorts, to help record some of the protocols, and what effect they had on Marley's cancer and for me to have something to do, to keep my mind busy and as a keepsake to show Marley later on in his life. Please forgive me for the inconsistent use of tenses, past and present, as sometimes I had to go back after a few days to fill the diary in.

After the diary section of Marley's last year, there is a short piece about my background, which is relevant to Marley's story. I added some stories of the people we have loved and lost from cancer and cancer treatment, also very relevant to Marley making his decision to find another way.

I added the protocols that Marley chose to heal his cancer and his new lifestyle after surgery and some recipes.

I put in some quotes, prayers and teachings that I follow every day, (sometimes it seemed all day), to keep me positive. I hope they will help any of you going through any of life's challenges. I still do them. They are part of me, who I am.

I have included personal letters to doctors and pieces from Marley's Dad, Andy, his brother Archie and sister Annabelle. I felt this book had to written from the whole family's perspective.

As an appendix, I have included the transcript from the WhatsApp group named Big Love that helped so much. It was such an important part of my life I could not leave it out.

Marley looking amazing, 22 days before he died. After surgery not one illness, not one visit to the doctor.

I love this picture with light emanating from him, in his new found serenity, in his last, but best year. You can just see the tattoo above his waist line of Triton (a Greek God and messenger of the sea) that he had out of respect for his cancer, also called Triton, the snake on his arm to represent transformation and my favourite "Never been better" on his other arm.

Chapter One - Boom your life changes

It made me laugh sitting in the chair talking to our GP. His coffee mug read "Please don't confuse your Google search with my medical degree". We all do it. Well my family does and my sister Clare thinks she is medically trained.

From the moment I saw my son in July 2017 and saw how emaciated he had become since seeing him in May, seemingly happy and healthy after finishing three years at University, I started researching on the internet. The worst thing for a worried parent is not being able to take action and researching gave me just that.

On the advice of his older flatmate, who had seen Marley's health and behaviour decline quickly, Marley came home. He knew something was very wrong. He had had earache and several trips to his GP down in Brighton.

Marley's best friend Dom, Marley centre, Archie, Marley's brother, Brighton May 2017.

Antibiotics did nothing and the prescribed painkiller Co-Codamol had made him really constipated. Then the stomach aches began. The GP did some blood tests and the results came back with raised indicator markers. These show inflammation and that something is wrong within the body. We have lots of normal proteins in our blood. When cancer is active it releases chemicals or signals that cause our normal systems to become more active and make more of some of the proteins. A similar thing happens in infections). Marley was not happy with the GP in Brighton and wanted to come home and see his family GP, the same one that had diagnosed Marley with NF1, Neurofibromatosis type 1.

How it all began

Gene Genie

At the age of 12 Marley was being signed off at the asthma clinic. He had not had an attack for some years. Our family doctor was giving him a thorough examination and paused quietly while removing the stethoscope from his ears. "I think Marley has NF1". (Neurofibromatosis) He showed me the café au lait marks under his arms and on his back, I had presumed they were just birthmarks. I had no idea what he was talking about. He gave me some information sheets and a referral to see geneticists. The diagnosis was confirmed by an eye exam and a phone call from my Aunty to say all four of her children had it. I had no idea about my cousins. I had passed down the faulty gene and I felt awful.

Chromosome 17 was the trouble and caused tumours to grow on nerve endings. It is quite common, affecting about one in every 3,000 people and symptoms vary greatly from person to person. My sister was also researching and sent a link of a brave and wonderful girl with NF1, doing a vlog, hospitalised all the time with her condition. Then I pressed 'Images'. The screen filled with pictures of different people, all colours, ages and nationalities with tumours all over their bodies, completely disfigured.

I sat and stared at these people, heart racing, shocked, terrified.

I decided to turn off the computer and cross each bridge as I came to it. I was told that Marley may never have anything more than the café au lait spots and maybe some learning difficulties. Clearly not the case when he passed his degree with a 2:1. And also, 12 years later, the oncologist told us that NF1 increases the chance of cancer.

I made the mistake of not going in the room with him and the doctor in July 2017, as my son was an adult of 24 and had lived independently for three years. Marley went through his symptoms, which now included no energy or appetite and disturbed sleep patterns, but because of his baggy clothes the doctor had not seen how thin he had become (54kilos) and Marley had not mentioned the rapid weight loss. I would have pointed that out immediately.

In the same week there were more blood tests and a different doctor who was alarmed at the results, calling for more blood tests.

Meanwhile, I was researching anorexia, depression and liver problems possibly caused by the "poor man's" vegan diet Marley was on. I sent copies of his blood results to my friend, an oncologist, and another who studies tumours; both said they did not see anything sinister. My gut told me otherwise.

In the next few weeks we spent the days with Marley lying in the summer sun, one of us with him at all times. We took to sleeping with him at night in the front room, lying on mats.

Marley's Dad Keeping vigil in the sunshine.

Hot water bottles to relieve the aches, Rescue Remedy, camomile tea and rubbing his feet seemed to calm and help Marley relax. I would research and think while he slept.

I sang old songs from his childhood; his little sister Annabelle would massage his back and shoulders. He refused television, films, Play Station and any form of music. All of the things he usually enjoyed. A friend suggested acupuncture, which really helped. Massage also helped and reflexology too. He just wanted silence, which of course was very hard going on our loud family, but sitting in silence, rubbing his feet, watching him sleep, just him and me, was, I would say a spiritual experience.

We went out to Browns restaurant in Cambridge for his 24th birthday in August 2017 and it was good to see him eat and do something normal, even though it was short-lived, due to stomach pain after.

Our family :Marley's 24th birthday. Andy, Annabelle, myself, Marley and Archie

Around this time a really good friend had suggested I make up a WhatsApp group chat so friends and family could keep up with what was happening with Marley. It grew as more people that loved us found out. I named it "Big Love". This group kept me afloat when I thought I might drown.

I had booked a week's break in a friend"s cottage in Norfolk long, before Marley's arrival home and was pleased when he said he would join us; but he was not comfortable there, grumpy and ill, so his Dad took him home early and he had to have more blood tests. When I arrived home everyone was out, so I unpacked and relaxed with a cup of tea until I got the call from A&E. The GP had booked an X-ray as a precaution and as a last resort in their investigation, as they could not find a cause for Marley's symptoms and because Marley had also mentioned he had had a cough for a while, not a hacking cough (just an annoying every now and then cough).

Shocking X-ray results

The X-ray showed a large mass above his left lung so they sent him straight away to a very busy A&E. Panic set in and I wanted to throw up. On the crazy drive there I had an argument with God, a good shout and scream in the car. Then I told myself that giving in to fear and panic was a negative reaction and whatever happened I had to remain positive. We were taken to the ward that deals with chest problems and waited, playing cards, watching Marley sleep. A very tired and young doctor explained so kindly what they had found and another consultant sent us home and started booking other tests. MRI and CT scans. We were learning a new vocabulary.

September 2017 passed in a blur of working amidst lots of different tests in different hospitals, tests results that came back inconclusive. The worst was an ultrasound-guided biopsy. It was the first time in my life I prayed out loud. It seemed to take forever. The doctor had to guide, by ultrasound, a tiny grabbing device into the top of the tumour, going in from his neck to extract some cells. Marley was so brave. I really thought I was going to have a heart attack watching my son in the chair with legs and arms shaking in pain, almost like being electrocuted, the doctor kneeling on him and not telling us what he was doing because he had to concentrate. It was barbaric and on the third attempt we both said "no more". After that for it also to be inconclusive was a real blow

Crossing bridges one at a time

It was a very challenging time. I was not just taking care of Marley. I had two other kids both in shock at their lives being turned upside down, and a business to run. Not just any business. I am a registered Childminder and I work with incredibly amazing, busy families. They were all so understanding of our situation, but these families depended on me. I had to carry on, keep strong and be vigilant, but take each day as it came and cross those bridges one by one. And I had to look after myself. I had to get enough sleep, vitamins and exercise. I took to riding my bike alone very early in the morning. I rode hard up the hills (when I write "hard" probably just a bit faster than a mobility scooter) and usually started crying at the top, but by the time I got home I felt better and ready for the day.

Marley said he needed space and quiet. Of course he did. He had lived away from us for three years after all. I agreed and put out thoughts to the universe to bring help. So the solution. I had taken Archie for a rare one to one breakfast at Bill's in Cambridge. We were catching up and I said how we needed some space for Marley and how the only place I could see working would be the Mill house owned by our friends. I took a sip of my coffee, looked up and who should walk in with their family but the friends we were talking about. On this journey I felt many times how our needs were met perfectly. I spoke to them there and then and she agreed without any hesitation, to let him stay in their separate mill house for a while. A lovely light place right on the river ,but more importantly in the same village. I enjoyed cleaning the little house and getting it ready.

His brother Archie moved in with him to keep an eye. It was a Godsend. Marley started cooking, making music again when up to it and eating a little more. We went to Cambridge and enjoyed buying him some new equipment and furnishings for the mill. I always enjoyed shopping with Marley. When he was little I would take just him late night grocery shopping. It was our time to catch up. I always tried to find time for each of them separately which was not easy. Birthday shopping was always a joy with him. He knew what he wanted and always chose the coolest clothes. This time was different. He was so humble and he didn't want me to spend any money, probably after being so broke in Brighton. He took a lot of persuading and eventually I just grabbed it all and went and paid.

Marley says "No" to chemo

We were referred to the sarcoma team at Addenbrookes Hospital in Cambridge, the hospital Marley was born in. My friend and client is also an oncologist there and I kept her informed about whom we were seeing. It was so good to have the reassurance of her knowing, professionally, the people we would meet. I just kept the mantras going in my head 'everything we need is always provided' and 'we are always in the right place at the right time'.

We know the hospital really well. They have saved my life four times; saved my husband's hand when he was poisoned, helped bring Annabelle and Marley into the world and at one point when the kids were all little I felt like I lived in A&E. But I was still shocked to walk down the hall that led to the "Oncology" waiting room. It's huge, the biggest I have ever seen. A massive "L" shape, seating maybe 60 on one side and another 30 or so on the other.

I felt a bit overwhelmed by the amount of gaunt and pale-looking people, many bald, some with masks to protect them from germs, some leaning on shoulders of loved ones and some slowly walking through, so used to the routine. There was a ticket machine for people waiting for bloods to be drawn. I wondered how my father-in-law, who was not a fan of hospitals, had felt walking into the waiting room for the first time on his own. He had literally just finished radiotherapy treatment for prostate cancer. It must have been really frightening.

The first member of our "A" team

We met the oncologist and the cancer nurse to talk through the findings of the PET-CT scan in a tiny, windowless room. We had a long discussion about the options available. Dr.Wong suspected it was a nerve sheath tumour. The good news was the cancer was nowhere else, it had not metastasised. He recommended chemotherapy, radiotherapy and surgery. Marley was already booked in at The Royal Papworth Hospital for removal but the doctor suggested, with much respect to the surgeons at Papworth, that we go to The Royal Brompton hospital in London as they were chest specialists. He also recommended a biopsy there. Marley asked for sedation, as he was not going to have the same agonising experience as last time. Marley also said he would not be having chemo or radiotherapy and the Doctor listened to Marley's reasoning. Marley was very young when my really good friend Jobug died from cancer and Marley witnessed the side effects from her treatment. The doctor told us his recommendations a few times, explaining in different ways, but saying the same thing. Surgery, chemo, radiotherapy. He felt very strongly in his beliefs about treatment, but Marley felt strong in his and reiterated his decision. The doctor finally accepted it and said that he felt Marley was too sick, too thin to have chemo anyway. We had a lot to think about but I was glad, looking at those poor people in the waiting room that chemo was not an option. I looked across at Marley and I was so proud of him, he looked serene, as he walked out of there, not a flicker of doubt or fear.

We had had weeks to talk about the worst-case scenario. I had to choose my moment to talk and sometimes out of the silence Marley would just come out with something deep and profound. I think he had faced the prospect of death, had known he was very ill and was OK with dying. So was I. I could only accept, survive and thrive (not survive be lying in a bed, still alive with heart beating, but sick and in pain, depressed and wishing for death).

I had said to Marley in an emotional rant that I would support his decisions no matter what. He would not be alone. We would be on the journey together. If he wanted to end his life I would take him to Switzerland, for assisted suicide. I do not believe in suffering. My school friend was diagnosed with cancer in his 30's and hanged himself. Marley reassured me he wouldn't do that.

Chris Wark...You legend!

In early 2017 my sister Clare had posted a story on Facebook of a husband talking about his wife who had been diagnosed with cancer, refused treatment and had gone on to live for quite a long time but who had just died and I remember thinking (sitting on a very high horse):"Well, if she had done the chemo she would still be here today!" Obviously I now completely understand what that guy was trying to convey. That she took control of her cancer and travelled her own journey and died with dignity, many years after diagnosis, with none of the side effects to deal with from treatment.

It was around this time my sister sent me a link for chrisbeatcancer.com, Chris Wark, an American guy who was diagnosed with stage 3 colon cancer in 2002, and who had surgery, also refused chemo and radiotherapy and put his survival down to radical lifestyle changes, nutrition and exercise. I typed it into Google and clicked on a link but the title was "Quackery didn't beat Chris Wark's cancer, Surgery did". So I read the article of criticism first anyway, which was a good thing. I agreed with the very angry surgeon that yes the cancer had been removed but then I thought keeping cancer from recurring is another thing.

I re-read it several times then went on to Chrisbeatcancer on YouTube and saw "20 things to ask your oncologist". I nearly wept with hope and relief to hear his candid, no nonsense, logical approach from his experience and from other survivors and it took all my gut-wrenching fear about cancer away. "You have time, the cancer has been there for a while, and you are not going to die straight away". Wow. I can't tell you how much it helped me remain positive. I viewed all of his posts and the videos of other survivors and their stories.

Carry on as normal

In late September we took Marley to dinner to celebrate his graduation. He didn't want to go back to university in Brighton for the ceremony. Marley was the first in our family to go to university apart from my grandfather and I was so proud. We had talked about the graduation ceremony previously and as usual Marley was nonplussed. His Aunty Clare had wanted to get him a graduation cap and gown. Now none of that seemed important but I wanted to mark the occasion as he had worked so hard to get that degree.

It was a really lovely evening, a pleasant distraction, and I think he enjoyed it.

Archie and Marley at his graduation celebration dinner 20th September 2017

I was trying to take Marley out as much as possible, to do normal things, like lunch out in Cambridge while we waited for each test result. I also wanted to get him to eat more to put some weight on.

Viva the Vagus Nerve

We had arranged to stay in London at the end of September at a friend's flat, yet another blessing for us. A beautiful, modern, light space right on the Thames by Tower Bridge. It was available at the time we needed it and rent-free. We went via taxi very early to our appointment at the Royal Brompton hospital for a biopsy. It was a beautiful morning, driving through London, but I was fearful that Marley's vagus nerve might be damaged during the procedure and was trying hard to keep calm and breathe through the worry. Sitting in the cab, enjoying the distraction of familiar landmarks, a story came on the radio of a young man, younger than Marley, doing really well at school, a friend to many, who was stabbed for no reason and died. I silently prayed for the family and got my life back into perspective.

I had never heard of the vagus nerve before but of course after the meeting with Dr Wong we researched. The vagus nerve is amazing. It runs from the brain, down the side, past his ears and face and neck, right down to the abdomen. It affects swallowing, speech, coughing and the digestive system, hence all of his initial symptoms and my worry of it being damaged in any way. At about the same time as Marley's diagnosis Stanley Rosenberg got his book published, "Accessing the Healing Power of the Vagus Nerve, self help exercises for anxiety, depression, trauma, and autism". Two hundred pages showing the importance of the nerve for psychological and physical well-being.

The 2nd member joins our "A" team

The Royal Brompton is a small hospital in Chelsea and we liked it there. So different from the ever-growing Addenbrooke's site that is almost a city in itself. In this little hospital, people knew and greeted each other. Staff shared banter along the corridors and smiled at us. We found our way to the ward and Marley was settled into a bed. A tiny lady with a very neat Khimar covering her head came in offering refreshments. We declined and said "nil by mouth". She asked us why we were there so we told her. She looked visibly moved and with a sweet smile said, "I will pray for you". Marley and I were very touched by her unexpected and welcome gesture in this new environment.

We had several setbacks, almost a comedy of errors. After waiting a long time we were told that the blood results had not been sent from Cambridge so the procedure could not be done. We just looked at each other in disbelief, but then we laughed and said in unison: "Everything for a reason". We did get to meet the surgeon, Miss Begum, and discussed the operation. We all liked her immediately and felt it had been worth the trip just to meet her. She stormed in with a backup team. Maybe they were used to getting abuse in giving patients such bad news. She was so young, wearing theatre scrubs and also quite small. She had a big voice though. She spoke fast and was absolutely furious that we had been inconvenienced. She ordered everyone around us to fix the problem. We talked about the procedure and the way she was going to go in to remove the tumour. I felt relief in having this young, brash and intelligent lady on our team.

A second biopsy, with a sedative a week later was successful and Marley came out of the room smiling and saying how different the experience had been. To see my son smile during that time was very rare and lifted my heart so much. Even if it was due to the drugs he was on.

Every setback we had worked in our favour by giving us more time to research, prepare for life after surgery and to get our team together. I sifted through a lot of suggestions for alternative protocols and was just as thorough reading them as with conventional treatment evidence. I read them out to Marley while he rested. I watched more YouTube testimonials from survivors. I started to learn about cancer and how to make the environment as unfriendly as possible for it to survive. People were getting their cancer to stop growing. They were living with cancer and some were clearing their body completely of cancer.

Resting and waiting around a lot in the Royal Brompton Hospital.

After the biopsy Marley wanted to see his friends in Brighton. His brother went too. I think they had a nice time, so much so that he didn't want to come home for the meeting with Dr Wong, so I decided to go on my own and see Dr Wong for the results of the biopsy and CT PET scan. I felt without Marley there I could ask the potentially very uncomfortable "20 questions to ask your oncologist." I had downloaded from the Chris Wark website.

The diagnosis

I didn't ask 20 questions, just a few that we needed answering and I knew some of those would be difficult to answer, but Dr Wong was great, open and spoke professionally but also from the heart. I was told it was a malignant nerve sheath tumour as predicted and because of the research I had done, I didn't get the shock that a lot of people experience. The tumour had been growing slowly for a while (which is exactly what Chris Wark had said about most cancers), then had had a spurt of growth which led to a necrotic (dead) centre. To me this had coincided with Marley finishing university when he was not sure what to do in his life after so long studying and worrying about money and his future. After a breakup in his relationship with his girlfriend Gracie. A lot of stress, in my mind, had lead to the growth spurt.

I was told that without treatment Marley would have a year to live. We had time.

I was told even with chemo and radiotherapy there was a 50% chance of recurrence, which worked in our favour really, no point considering chemo with those chances.

Time to Cross that Bridge

I thanked the doctor and left giving him a smile, and I did say I felt sorry for him having to be the one to tell me. I really did feel blessed having Dr Wong on our team. I asked for the names of the drugs he wanted to use and researched all the background on returning home, such as the five and ten year survival rates, history of the drugs, the side effects.

Doxorubicin was first used in 1969. Hardly the new, ground-breaking drug that I was hoping for. It is used to treat many cancers and the side effects were listed on three sides of an A4 leaflet. They included heart failure; second cancer; damage to the heart muscle; hair loss; liver changes; increase risk of infection and nausea.

Ifosfamide was first approved for use in 1987. Again, side effects covered three sides of an A4 leaflet. They included similar side effects as Doxorubicin and the two drugs used together also had side effects of liver and kidney damage; confusion and hallucinations; loss of appetite and nausea; mouth ulcers and bladder irritation.

After thinking, researching and drinking a lot of coffee, praying for the right words to use and rehearsing my speech, I spoke to Marley on the phone in Brighton. I told him as gently as I could it was cancer and malignant. Without a pause Marley said, "well I know it's cancer but I want to stay a bit longer in Brighton".

I told him to stay however long he wanted and to have fun. He had known it was cancer. I had remained ever hopeful that it was not cancer until it was told to me directly. I smiled at Marley's amazing, calm reaction and attitude. I could not have been prouder of my son at that moment.

A welcome celebration in the midst of a crisis

My niece, also named Gracie, had her 21st birthday party in October 2017, a massive event in the village hall with hundreds of family members coming from all over England and flying in from New Zealand to celebrate with us, and what a blessing they were to us all. They showed us so much love. In the weeks leading up to the party they entertained Annabelle and Archie so I needn't worry about them so much, which took some of the pressure off my shoulders, knowing they were happy and looked after.

I didn't expect Marley to come on the day of the party. He never really attended family get togethers, but he did arrive and surprisingly stayed a long time into the night. I remember plastering on the make up as it was the first time I was going to see a lot of people since the diagnosis and I felt really fragile. I really was on the edge. It was a brilliant party. The highlight was the New Zealand family's heartfelt speeches and a display of old photos of the family followed by a powerful and emotional Haka. There was so much love in that hall all day, surrounding us. The next morning at

41

breakfast, my cousin Mandy very tentatively gave Marley some information on different supplements and protocols. Mandy works with racehorses, helping with rehabilitation after injury or illness and corrective nutrition. She does a lot of research and is very knowledgeable. Marley was interested and in good spirits.

Everyone came in together for breakfast and friends turned up unexpectedly from the village just to help serve and clear. We talked and ate. It was a perfect respite weekend and really lifted our spirits.

Just another ride on the worst Rollercoaster

We were given a date for the operation to remove the tumour and again arranged with our friends to stay in their flat. We took Marley for a lung function test at the sister site round the corner, over the road from the famous Royal Marsden that we had heard such a lot about, from Aunty Joy's cancer treatment.

We were given a date for Marley's surgery in late October, to remove the tumour. They had to make sure Marley was fit and well for the operation by giving him a lung function test at the Old Brompton hospital. We really liked it. A beautiful building. We were imagining Victorian nurses rustling along the corridors in their long skirts. It seemed empty. The staff were wonderful, a really swift and efficient service, but I had already been given a little experience of the non-communication between departments. I made a point of taking the results with us instead of them being posted to the surgical team, as the operation was due to take place the following Monday. I was glad I had when on meeting Miss Begum at the pre-op meeting straight after the lung function test, she asked for the results and rejoiced on our producing them.

Everything looked good and we settled Marley in his side room at the Brompton on the Sunday. Me and Andy went back to the flat. I spent the night praying, listening to music and looking out at the Thames and reading WhatsApp messages posted for Marley on "Big Love".

After an early start to get back to the Brompton on time, we sat and waited with Marley, looking out over Chelsea. Miss Begum came rushing in and said brashly

"Marley are you well? Your bloods are not good, your iron levels are really low and your inflammation markers are up". We looked bemused at each other, what the hell? So more tests would have to be done to make sure Marley was fit enough for a safe operation.

Lifted out of the water by the Big Love boat

When Miss Begum and her entourage left the room we were silent and in shock. Marley didn't even look at us and said, " I want you both to go." My heart broke a little, a small painful tear. We took the elevator in silence, reached the main entrance also in silence. My husband Andy walked one way and I walked the other, straight over the road to St Luke's, such a beautiful church. I sat in an aisle behind a column and sobbed. Big Love was with me though and the messages of comfort came flooding in. I prayed and cried until eventually Andy came and found me and gave me a poppy. He had memorised all the history of the church and told me a story of a French man in a hot-air balloon getting caught on the spire who fell to his death in the road outside the hospital. I felt so wretched it made me laugh out loud at my husband's terrible way of cheering me up. We decided to walk around London to pass the time.

We walked up to Hyde Park, past the monument to Prince Albert and had lunch by the Serpentine. The sun was shining and although we felt emotionally spent it was a

beautiful walk. All the while Big Love was sending pictures and texts.

As well as Big Love keeping us afloat, we saw positive signs everywhere. This was on a wall in Chelsea.

We carried on walking to Buckingham Palace. The red leaves from the ancient trees inside the royal grounds had started to fall and made a vibrant carpet on the ground. I picked one up to keep and press. Marley called. He had had time to process the news of another operation delay and sounded relaxed. It was such a relief. So we walked back to see him. He was to have antibiotics, an iron infusion and had to stay put, hopefully to have the operation on the following Thursday. So the week waiting for his bloods to get better, was spent going backwards and forwards to the hospital. His appetite had increased so we bought him vegetable juices and baguettes on the way to visit, then ordered food delivery most evenings. He was an eating machine. The staff all became familiar faces and were really wonderful to Marley, keeping him in the side room, which was such a Godsend as everyone else on the main ward had terrible problems with their chests, all coughing and in pain and all much older than Marley.

Number 3 joins the healing team

I found researching non-toxic healing protocols a challenge. There was so much information and conflicting evidence. I felt overwhelmed and wanted an expert to help guide us.

I had asked a friend and client to advise us early in October as she had just completed a degree in nutrition, but she turned us down, not confident to help us with healing cancer. She did however give us her tutor's number who she highly recommended, Dr Xandria Williams. I read all of her published work, listened to her podcasts, and watched all of her videos of conferences beforehand.

I arranged a meeting with Dr Williams. She was based around the corner from the Brompton in Sloane Square. Our friends helped us pay her fees. We took a taxi as I wasn't sure Marley would be up to the walk. Xandria's office was huge, with high ceilings and it reminded me of my grandparents living rooms filled with art, books piled everywhere and mismatched fabrics in rich colours. It was reassuring to talk things through with someone so experienced.

It was a whirlwind 30 minute meeting and before we knew it we were being shown down a tiny, narrow, stairwell to an office with supplements lining the walls.

Suddenly, Marley stopped halfway down and held his head, his eyes shut tight in pain. I got him to sit down on the stairs. I could feel my adrenalin kicking in, my heart racing, what the hell was happening? Meanwhile, a young assistant was carrying on regardless, asking me questions about which products we needed and telling me how much they were. Maybe she was so used to very sick people visiting. "Just the lot, whatever Dr Williams said", I barked. I didn't care about anything else just my boy sitting on the stairs in severe pain. All I could tell him was to breathe through the pain, to keep breathing. It lasted quite a few minutes then it vanished, and Marley came back to me. He said it had been like someone stabbing him through his skull with a knife and that it was awful. I presumed it was nerve pain caused by the tumour. When we left I wasn't thinking straight and made him walk past the taxi rank around the other side of the square like an idiot, people bustling past us going about their business while my world was in slow motion. We got back to the hospital and I was so glad to be back there near the medical team. My legs started to shake with delayed shock and worry.

We'd learnt a lot about cancer cells in the meeting with Dr Williams and it seemed that what I had been feeding him to get the calories up was basically feeding the cancer. So we stopped all sugar, all the baguettes and take-a-ways and I took him in more cold-pressed vegetable juices and salads. I was now researching all the supplements that I hadn't had time to ask about in the meeting with Dr Williams.

So we left the hospital with Marley and once again our friends let us stay in their beautiful, open plan flat, overlooking Tower Bridge and the Thames. It was so calm and relaxing. Some days I felt as if I were bobbing about in the Bermuda Triangle and only kept afloat with the messages, photos, quotes and prayers on Big Love. Within the week Marley's white blood cell count went down, which was a good thing and he started to look better. Archie and Annabelle came for a couple of days and there was a welcome visit from old friends from Twickenham and Andy's cousin Sharon. His ex-girlfriend Gracie came and stayed at the flat with us. She had to take herself out on to the balcony for a moment as she had not seen Marley for a while and was shocked and saddened by his appearance and sickness. Gracie was a breath of fresh air. She helped fill in a huge questionnaire from the naturopath. We watched fireworks on the river together from the balcony and I was so happy to have her with us. We relaxed and watched River life, researching while Marley rested.

A

welcome visitor, Gracie, helping me fill in the questionnaire from the naturopath. Marley looking out over the Thames.

Gracie left us after a few days for Brighton and we went back into the Brompton, both calm. My friend Lisa came to visit me in transit from Dubai. It was so unexpected and so welcome to see a friend from normal life. I could not believe she had gone to so much trouble to see me. We had lunch together around the corner from the hospital. We chatted, laughed and cried.

Marley the day before the operation.

Marley wanted to be alone the night before the operation and I accepted that. I prayed and was carried through with "Big Love" ever present. Andy and I slept well, listened to music and kept calm and positive, but were silent at the time we knew he would be wheeled down to theatre. We made our way over to him after a visit to HMS Belfast to distract us and afterwards we prayed in St Luke's. The operation took six hours. I couldn't wait to speak to Miss Begum to find out how it went. The surgeons had had a tough job. They got out the tumour even though it had grown since the last MRI and it ruptured on removal.

The vagus nerve had to be cut a little but they were confident that he would be OK. I wept with relief and hugged the team. I think I had held my breath through the whole of the debriefing.

A selfie with Miss Begum after the operation, Andy and one of the team. We were so happy that the vagus nerve had not been damaged and Marley was OK.

Marley was brought back to the high-dependency unit and they took great care of him. Very rapidly they changed all his tubes over from theatre to bedside care. The speed and concentration to get it right was obvious and we stood back trying to keep out of the way. Marley talked to us, completely off his head on drugs, but he said he immediately felt better and that he had a tube up his penis, which definitely broke the tension. We were exhausted and emotionally drained but remained positive throughout. We left late into the night and as we returned to the flat the doorman came out to ask for news of Marley. So many very kind people, practically strangers, all thinking and praying for our boy.

The staff had Marley walking the next day, which I couldn't quite believe, but I trusted that magnificent team to know what they were doing. It was like seeing him walk for the first time as a baby. We were delighted, happy parents, and so proud of his resilience and determination.

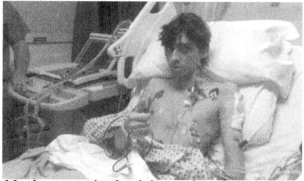

Marley, amazingly giving a thumbs up.

The healing begins

The next week Andy decided to return home to look after the kids and to sort Marley's room and to make it bigger.

Even though I knew Archie and Annabelle were being watched over by family and friends in the village, and that they were more than capable of taking care of the house, puppy and themselves, we felt that one of us needed to go and check in with them.

I got into a routine of visiting every day and seeing Marley improve little by little. A different tube removed each time. The after-effects of surgery and the side- effects of the drugs used were a worry. I kept this at bay with affirmations and prayers and Marley grew stronger. He started itching from the morphine and his arm was swollen due to the surgery, but thankfully it went down again. He was meant to be discharged within the week but he was not ready and he told me so. I agreed, so we spoke to Miss Begum and the team and he stayed for another week which was a big relief.

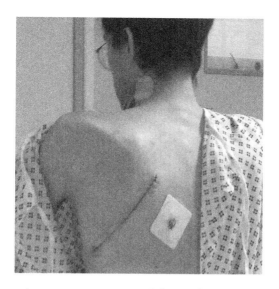

A very neat scar and lung drains.

Marley started eating. And I mean like a horse. It was so wonderful after so long watching him in pain and uncomfortable and with no appetite. I spent the days looking out at the Thames in the morning and researching, buying food, traveling to the Brompton, buying more food, researching on the laptop and reading up, cross-referencing all that the naturopath had told us and writing out thank-you cards for the staff and, of course, Miss Begum. As Marley left there were lots of lengthy goodbyes to the staff. The night before we came home we had to stay in hospital accommodation as our friend needed the flat back. The accommodation was a big change and pretty awful compared to the luxury pad. Juggling luggage, medications, supplements and a recovering Marley, who was still very weak was a huge challenge and a huge responsibility. I carried on with my affirmations in my head when I felt stressed and Big Love kept me laughing when my humour failed. I was so grateful that I had not had to stay all those weeks in that small, soulless, detergent-smelling dwelling. I felt sorry for the families we passed in the corridor all looking tired and worried.

Homecoming

On the 17th November we took a taxi home, thank goodness. It would have broken me physically and mentally trying to protect Marley from getting bumped on public transport. We had used the same taxi firm back and forth to the flat. It was expensive, but pre-operation, Marley was too ill to manage public transport and we liked all the drivers. It was good to meet different people and hear about their lives, and it gave us something else to think about other than Marley's cancer.

We arrived home on Andy's birthday. A very quiet and calm homecoming. We were all emotional and happy.

The early days at home were a challenge too. Marley had decided to move back home from the millhouse in the village whilst in London. His annex in the garden wasn't ready yet, so he had the sofa, which was not ideal. I moved rooms around and had a good sort-out. I had taken some time off work but needed to get working again. Marley busied himself with organising his meds, doctors' appointments and juicing. He felt so much better. The symptoms making his life a misery had disappeared. There were a few minor worries, swellings in his hand and feet but they went down after a few days. As soon as he felt able he went back to Brighton to see his friends for a few days. He cut down his painkillers as soon as he could and we started looking for a personal trainer. From our research we knew how critical exercise would be in his recovery and in stopping the cancer recurring.

I went back to work in December and it was wonderful to see all the kids again. I felt I could breathe once more and even went out with a friend to a Christmas fundraiser. I hadn't drunk alcohol for months and the pre-going-out Cosmopolitan went down very nicely.

Number 4 of the A team comes to our door

Sam a personal trainer from CrossFit, came into our lives on such a terrible day. Marley had decided to come off morphine without telling me. I was busy working. Andy came downstairs and said Marley was not right. I got Andy to sit with the kids and went to find Marley upstairs. He was having a complete mental breakdown and was in the depths of despair. I sat down on the floor at the top of the stairs next to him. Marley's outpouring of emotion, probably bought on by morphine withdrawal, was truly awful to witness and my heart ripped open. I listened to all he had to say. With the help of hugs, empathy, reassurance and love he calmed. His Dad and I did a tag team of love to get him through. Peppa pig helped out by occupying the children, but I texted all the parents and they came and got the children early without any hesitation.

I had contacted Sam through a friend and he said he would pop in for a chat at some point. Sam came and knocked at the door, post morphine crisis. A massive hulk of a guy with a beard and a warm smile. I was a bit embarrassed at the state of the house and I was a little shaky still and looked shocking no doubt. He was so positive, kind and enthusiastic. He went off and found other protocols and new information from a professional friend and coach. Over the coming weeks he worked closely and carefully with Marley to give him the confidence to exercise on his own. He never took a penny from us. Yet another everyday angel that came into our lives and lifted us.

Three months post-operation February 2018

Marley is strong, strict on himself with the protocols, doing yoga CrossFit, juicing and supplements, starting to make plans for his future, thinking of going on holiday. He has been painting, cooking, visiting museums, making music and seeing his old friends.

Marley making bread, February 2018

Four months post op March 2018

Marley came in to the kitchen and showed me his stomach. He was concerned as lots more pea-sized tumours had come up. He always had had about six or seven, but he now had about 25 appear in a very short time. I took some photos for future reference and reassured him I thought they were NF1 lumps and not cancer. He decided to go back to Dr Wong. I went back to the NF1 drawing board and researched away, looking for any new treatments or breakthroughs. There is no known cure for NF1 and Marley's cancer had grown in one of the little tumours. I went back to Big Love as someone on there had mentioned a friend who was also a parent of an NF1 child and very knowledgeable. I got the contact numbers and spent a long time on the phone to two parents, one being an Ambassador for the Childhood Tumour Trust and it was lovely to be able to talk to someone, but also hard at the same time. They were impressed with my research and the fact Marley was trying a new protocol of Cannabidiol, or CBD oil topically, to see if it made any difference in reducing the size of the fibromas on his stomach.

After I had had time to digest all the new information and the stories the parents had shared with me, I became emotional and angry that Marley was having to deal with keeping cancer away and now the NF1 had decided to accelerate in numbers. FFS!

Dr Wong confirmed that they were NF1 fibromas and referred Marley to a specialist in London, but from talking to the NF1 parents, Marley thought it would be just for monitoring his NF1. Marley decided to cancel the referral.

Marley joined CrossFit tonight and it's great to watch him do pull ups and hand stands, just brilliant.

Five months post op April 2018

So tomorrow Marley and I are going back to Dr Wong to get CT results. He has already rung to say that Marley has a small blood clot in his lung, probably from the operation. He recommended blood thinners. I haven't asked Marley if he has started taking them. Tomorrow is going to be interesting to see if all the protocols have worked, and kept the cancer from returning. I feel calm and Marley seems to be in good spirits. He met with Tracey from CLIC Sargent , a charity introduced to us at the hospital who provide support for anyone under 25 with cancer. They went out for a cup of tea and a chat which did him good.

One day at a time! Miracle follows miracle and wonders never cease.

Marley helping out my charges with some Lego building. April 2018

The conclusion from the meeting was that the cancer journey is not over just yet. It has taken me a while to process and get my positive pants back on. Actually that didn't take long, maybe overnight, but life got in the way of me writing. When you have a family anything can happen and the night before the meeting with Dr Wong I was woken at maybe one in the morning with my daughter having problems with her circle of friends, the usual crap that goes on between teenage girls and she was worried. I wish I could say I was an understanding, patient mother but I did my best to listen even though Madre, (the term my kids refer to me sometimes) is not good when deprived of sleep. I decided to take Annabelle with us to the CT results meeting. I asked Marley first. I wanted Annabelle to witness what her brother had to go through and to put some perspective on the "He said, she said" crowd that was upsetting her.

It was a beautiful spring day, the first sun we had had in such a long time and as we sat in the oncology waiting room I was thinking, wow what a difference a sunny day makes. All the staff were smiling and even the patients looked cheery. Annabelle noticed the good spirits too.

We were shown into the same small, white room with a tiny window up high. After introductions I knew it was not going to be the miraculous recovery we had hoped for. Dr Wong does not have a "poker face". The cancer nurse now joined us and then yet another nurse who we had not met before (six people now in that cosy space). The doctor started with the warning that we already knew about the blood clots and the reason for the medication. Then a short pause as he chose his words carefully.

A lesson of patience, taught by the child

They thought the cancer had come back at the site of the original tumour. They suggested chemotherapy again and Marley said he had not changed his mind and refused the treatment. Marley asked a lot of questions and then yet again for the third time (she liked to ask every time she saw Marley) the cancer nurse asked why? What were his reasons for refusing? Then she said, without looking at us, "I know you have lost a lot of loved ones, sorry about that" but her dismissive body language and lack of eye contact did not match her words. With the recent death of Aunty Joy (I will talk about her later), still raw in my heart I felt like strangling that nurse at that moment and telling her how I felt when Joy told me she had lost her hearing overnight from the last round of chemo and all the other horrific side effects she had suffered in the last 8 years. I held it in and kept quiet.

Marley paused and took his time with his response. "I feel that this world is a big place, big enough to offer more than just three treatments to heal". Surgery, chemotherapy and radiotherapy. He went on to talk about some of the alternative protocols and the response from the medics was of concern about being careful and that some could be dangerous. Marley was well aware that just because something is natural it does not mean it is not toxic. I looked at him, all the while thinking who is this Buddha-like guy talking with so much calmness, at peace with the world and showing great understanding towards these fearful nurses?

They wanted to book him in anyway and said he could cancel later but again he quietly but firmly declined. Then the other nurse butted in and said, "You'd better hurry up, it is growing." Wow!

So I stated calmly (but inside my heart was beating faster in anger over her fear-mongering) "As there was no baseline scan as such, how do you know it is growing?" She did not know.

Both nurses now were adding their opinions and I couldn't help my finger pointing as I said. "That is your belief, not Marley's".

Marley cut in and asked calmly for a scan in six weeks so we would know for sure. A sensible suggestion and it bought the meeting to a conclusion. As we walked out Annabelle said how she thought the nurses had put up a good argument. I did not answer as I was furious and told Annabelle with a smile to wait with Marley while I got the car. I called Andy and did a big blubbery rant and cry and then I was perfectly calm by the time I picked them up. I hid a lot of emotion behind my sunglasses.

Later Marley said how he thought I hadn't handled the meeting very well (if only he knew the angry volcanic eruption I had suppressed inside my head) and that I should be more understanding of the fact that chemo and radiotherapy treatment was all the doctors and nurses knew and they believed in it. I accepted the telling off and knew he was right and will try to be more like Marley in future! On the way home Marley started talking about what he wanted to try next.

Cannabis oil and cannabis refugees

I had been doing more research on cannabis oil and I knew this would probably be the next protocol Marley would choose, as we had discussed a plan B. There is a lot of information on this protocol on the internet and a lot on the news at the moment. A lady called Joy Smith had healed herself from cancer with the oil and is now joining the fight to legalise medical cannabis in this country. I have signed petitions online, looking at images of children and desperate parents who can see a positive difference in their children's health (for epilepsy too) when they start administering the oil. But they can't get it on prescription, it is not cheap and also illegal.

I had also spoken to some elderly gentlemen in the village before Marley was diagnosed. These two wonderful husbands and carers told me that friends of friends had got them some cannabis which they made into cakes, they had given it to their wives, both suffering from Parkinson's disease and both had seen an improvement but were too scared to get the oil themselves. Heartbreaking really.

When you start looking, it is amazing to find a whole new world of survivors and wonderful people trying to share their story and help others. Rick Simpson, a Canadian man, has helped over 5,000 people heal themselves using his unique cannabis oil concentrate free of charge, after healing himself of several ailments (in 1997) including skin cancer by applying the oil topically. He is great to watch in his videos, very matter of fact, like the old guys on the DIY self help videos. He helps people for no monetary gain and perseveres to spread the news of his findings and has to deal with people slating his work a lot of the time.

Marley could travel to where cannabis is legal (they call themselves cannabis refugees) but here, in England he can be monitored by Dr Wong and live for free (rent paid, he can obtain organic fruit and veg, supplements etc.) with us. He has applied for several jobs but unsuccessfully. To this date he has still not received any money for being unable to work from the Government.

So we got the oil from overseas. He started the protocol last night as it only came yesterday. Waiting for it to arrive was a challenge of patience for me, as we only have four weeks now until the CT scan, but Marley was completely calm and accepting as usual. He ingests it like a supplement by decanting the oil into capsules. He will write detailed notes on how he gets on and now on day 2 his eyes are not so red, a side effect of the oil, which is a relief.

My cousin, Mandy sent me a documentary series called "The Truth about Cancer". I had heard about it from Chrisbeatcancer. I was a little put off with some of the sensationalism in the first episode about the history of the pharmaceutical companies. The experts and doctors from all over the world were interviewed on all sorts of diseases, not just cancers, and the different protocols and the testimonials of survivors were extremely interesting. I was searching for people healing themselves with cannabis oil and there were a few survivors in the UK interviewed that used cannabis oil. The same things came up every time. The problem of obtaining an illegal substance and getting the dosage right. It was alarming to see all the statistics on conventional cancer treatment results, the way the governing bodies in the US manipulate the results, so on paper it looks like they are doing a good job when in fact the results are poor. Also, learning about the biochemistry and the importance of the functions of our cells that are damaged by conventional treatments, makes me very glad that Marley chose the path less travelled.

All together now

This last couple of weeks in April, I have been really looking at my other two kids' diets and lifestyles. Annabelle has had exams and the pressure is building, her skin is a mess, she is intolerable before her period, she craves sugar, processed, fast food and it is rare that she eats a vegetable. So we had a discussion and she was open to have a go at making things better and so far has really taken things on board, taking responsibility for changing her diet.

Archie and Annabelle

She wakes up slightly earlier. Fills a big water bottle up for the day. I make her a juice every day and at first I was making it with sweet fruits and a few greens but after a week she requested more veggies. So now she has carrot, ginger, lemon, apple, blueberries, spinach and a tiny amount of secret kale that she says she hates!! Her skin has improved and I think her mood too and exams week has not been hell. My son Archie is working like crazy, doesn't get enough sleep and doesn't make time to eat properly. He has had a chronic ear problem for years and has been to the GP several times. He says his hearing feels like he is under water, he sounds constantly bunged up, like something is obstructing his sinuses so we also had a talk and he now has a juice each day, plenty of water and a spoonful of chopped ginger and vitamins. It will be interesting to see how he feels in a couple of weeks.

Keeping busy

I believe that it is important to live each day fully and with Marley not being at work it is even more important to keep him busy living. Marley loves cooking so every other week we put on a supper for friends and family at our house. He spends the day before shopping and prepping, experimenting with herbs and tastes. The food is always good and always vegan. He works hard, clears up after himself and will socialise for a little while before going to relax in his little garden room.

He is researching all the time and this week he is looking into the diet and lifestyles of vegan, super-fit men, with quite incredible stories. He is also studying fasting. He has changed his protocols to include enemas again. I keep going back to the research and there is something I do not understand. If you are going to the toilet, two or three times a day, why is there a need for an enema? I know it stimulates the liver to produce an enzyme that is great in detoxing but how then do you keep the nutrients in that you are getting from the fresh food? I guess the nutrients are absorbed quickly because of the juicing.

Marley's delicious vegan pizza

Six Months Post Op. May 2018

Marley has been lucky enough to be under the care of Clik Sargent, a charity based at Addenbrookes hospital. They listen, help Marley access financial help and fill in forms. It gets Marley out and their kindness is humbling. They are trying to help Marley with finances as it is a very unfair system. If Marley had chemo or radiation treatment he would be getting more funding right now. Crazy when he has saved the NHS thousands of pounds, possibly hundreds of thousands. The doctor wanted to send us both out to Florida for Marley to have proton therapy, (a type of radiation therapy). Marley declined, but asked if he could have the money instead for his protocols. They smiled, apologised and declined his request.

Last night I spoke on the phone to a cancer survivor!! After watching so many stories on YouTube it was overwhelming to speak to an actual survivor. She is a volunteer on the helpline at the "Yes to Life" organisation. It was halfway through a long conversation that she told me she was a survivor herself. I cried. Four times she had healed herself. Healed four different cancers. Amazing.

She gave me information on another helpful organisation called "Fighting Cancer Together". We are hoping to access the charity to get free organic vegetables!! So happy right now. Tomorrow Marley is going back for another CT scan. I wanted him to put it off as he has not been on the cannabis protocol fully. There a delay in getting it and a delay between doses but he is happy to go to the scan. I am not afraid; I don't know how he feels.

Archie, myself and Marley at Aunty Pam's 80th in May 2018

7 Months Post. June 2018

Marley went for the results of his scan this morning. I stayed home as he didn't want me to go. He went with the lovely lady from CLIC Sargent and another, also lovely, lady from the Macmillan charity. I was engaged with outdoor learning in the woods with three little ones when he called. The oncologist was really pleased to see no further growth on the previous tumour site. Marley's bloods came back all normal. The cancer had not metastasised to his blood or to any other organ. The doctor was interested to hear what Marley had been doing, said nothing further of chemotherapy and told Marley to carry on with what he was doing. They did agree that his weight was now at minimal level. Marley had been, for the past two weeks, trying out fasting, after a lot more research. He wanted to try it out because by eating in the evening, juicing at lunch and having green tea and water at breakfast, leaving a longer gap between eating meals, the good cells would be more able to attack the bad cells and get rid of them. So we bought some new scales and Marley became very good at making detailed notes of all his protocols.

Marley researching and cross referencing June

2018

Gracie and Marley cooking for us, 7 months post op

Knowing when to celebrate

I cried lots of happy tears on hearing the good news, tears of joy for my son who has been quietly determined, taken on board everything he has researched and learned. In the middle of the woods, with the kids, hearing this wonderful news, who should appear from nowhere but the Reverend from my church. She stood quietly until I had finished the short conversation with Marley then gave me the biggest hug. It was very welcome.

After his previous results not being so positive, Marley had not been discouraged or disheartened. He just dusted himself down and changed course. He never got angry with the cancer nurses or hospital nutritionist for their views on cancer treatment and has quietly shown them that if you are willing to take responsibility for your disease, accept it and do all you can to research and try different things, after all, different protocols work for different people. We were now looking at a CT scan that showed no recurrence of the cancer.

Do not be discouraged. Release fear.

You can heal yourself.

I told his little sister the good news as she was coming home from school. She shouted it out to everyone on the bus and a cacophony of "Whoop, whoop" and "Yays".

She burst out crying too. His brother and Dad like me had full belief in Marley. We are all still smiling.

I told Big Love as I hadn't posted anything for ages. As usual I was bombarded with wonderful positive messages .

Marley will go back to the hospital in August for another scan.

When I got back from the woods with the kids, I asked Marley how he felt. He said that he felt sure of this protocol but when something confirms your belief it's amazing. I told him, half blubbering in joyful tears, how proud I am of him and that he knows far more than me about life and death at 24 than I know at 50 and maybe he had found the meaning of life…to want to go on and help other people.

We went to CrossFit together this morning and saw Sam and had hugs. Huge smiles were on our faces. All of us, all day.

Second from the right is Sam, myself, Patrick an old friend, and Marley at CrossFit

In June I saw one of my best friends who, in the previous October, gave me money from her and her husband to spend on anything the NHS couldn't fund. Basically that's everything when you say "No" to chemo. I was overwhelmed with relief at the time and still am. I thought it would last six months at least, it lasted three months and saw us through. Thank God, as we were already in debt. When you are dealing with crisis management and it's your kid, then money, debt, doesn't matter. I learnt to say "F*ck it" quite a lot about finances. Other relatives and friends did kindly give us a few hundred pounds here and there and it came at times when I was saying affirmations daily for money to come as we were at the wire and it came. Just enough to pay the rent or buy some supplements, so we have been so lucky and blessed. We can never repay our friend's kindness unless, this book becomes a bestseller. Haha!

Marley asked at the time how we could ever repay them? I did not know and when he said it again this morning, after pausing and thinking about our friends, I said "Survive and thrive, live a good life and help others".

He will carry on with the cannabis protocol for another two weeks. He will continue exercising, nourishing his body, remain vigilant for changes in his body, weight, sleep patterns and visual signs. He said he may volunteer in a charity shop after he has visited his friends in Brighton this week. Still doing a day a time but he is once again thinking about what to do next. How wonderful that I can write that...........

Marley left and Archie making juice in July 2018 and below enjoying a walk in Coploe pit.

Gracie and Marley in Brighton July 2018

Eight months post operation. July 2018

With the school term coming to an end and it being nearly a year since Marley came home, I was thinking about holidays. Annabelle and I are going to climb Snowdon. I love Wales, the landscape and the air. In the planning I felt distracted and concerned about Marley. He is fasting and although remaining the same weight, to me he doesn't look quite as vibrant as he did in June. So yesterday, after he had had a wonderful time with his Grandma, reading and discussing life, I told him how I felt. He said he has had aches and pains lately and maybe lost confidence at CrossFit. He said he felt maybe the tumour was either growing, (I believe is perfectly normal thinking for any survivor to think any new pain is cancer), or perhaps it is scar tissue from all the tubes he had in his side to drain his lungs. Marley said he had not felt very good lately and maybe he had overdone it in training. I showed him the video of him rowing at CrossFit, maybe eight weeks post op, and how strong he looked then. This journey is all about taking stock and adapting if need be and changing course. I am looking forward to him finishing the cannabis protocol as I believe it has done the job we wanted it to do and now he needs to be without it, to move on and not hide behind a smokescreen, so to speak as I think this maybe detrimental to his healing. He is spending a lot of time with his Grandma, who had a terrible car accident in which a cyclist was seriously injured. She is feeling really awful. She has lost her driving licence as a consequence and faces a court hearing. We are all devastated for her as she has spent her whole life helping people in her personal life and in her long career in social services. Marley has taken on a carer and chauffeur role and it is good for both of them. I asked Marley if he wanted to go to see a counsellor and he said, "why should we pay for that when I have Grandma?". But whenever he has a down moment, or I see a visible sign of a pain or an ache, my stomach flips and I don't want to go on holiday or be anywhere away from him. This must be a normal feeling. Marley had also been sent the latest clinic letter from Dr Wong, outlining their last meeting. Although his bloods were clear and there was no regrowth, Dr Wong used the words: "This is a recurrent disease and is inoperable and without chemotherapy the disease could progress."

Marley painting and relaxing in the garden
July 2018

Marley didn't paint before his diagnosis. Afterwards, he found it relaxing and it kept his mind busy. We all followed suit and started to do more art together

Nine months post op. July 2018

I could sense a change in Marley and by the middle of August I wished we didn't have to wait until the end of the month for another CT scan. As suspected, the CT scan at the end of the month showed regrowth of a 9cm mass on the previous tumour site. In the meeting Marley was thoughtful, asked questions and listened quietly. He only showed emotion when the Macmillan support lady didn't show up as a replacement for Tracy from CLIC Sargent, who would have never missed a meeting. The replacement Macmillan lady was thrown in at the deep end and didn't know Marley or anything about him. He welled up and quietly said, "Lets go". After thanking the doctor we left quickly. On the walk back to the car he announced he was going to Ibiza and later booked a flight leaving in a few days' time. I was in shock and did not know what to say so said nothing. All feeling seemed to leave me. He asked me what would happen if he died there. I said, "Ibiza is a nice island and we would bury you there if need be and don't worry about dying, just go and do whatever you need to do".

We argued a lot that following week, nothing was right, everything was wrong and I was glad he went away to be honest, as I felt overwhelmed, worn out and totally crap at everything. One morning we had an argument about vegan pancakes. I was doing my best to create something that resembled a tasty blueberry pancake but they were rubbish, even after several attempts. He was so angry and mean. I just walked out and went up to Coploe pit, a disused chalk pit up the hill near our house and cried and cried for hours by myself. At all the frustration, the anger, the unfairness of life, the cruel twists and turns of Marley's young life that he had to deal with and feeling sorry for myself.

I argued with God again. I knew Marley wasn't following the protocols 100% and I was scared. I shouted, "God what is it I need to do?" A resounding *Do nothing!* came back. I stood in shock and questioned the answer that came to me. What do you mean, do nothing? The hardest thing for me ever to do was to do nothing. I didn't know why Marley was not following his protocols 100%. Maybe it was because a small fibroma was visible on his forehead and even if he got rid of this cancer, it would be a lifelong healing quest as new tumours appeared. Or maybe the pressure on the nerve was dragging his motivation down. I won't   ever   know. When I came back down the hill he gave me a hug immediately and said how sorry he was. I am sure he was processing the information given to him at the hospital and he   was   lost   emotionally.   Someone recommended a session with a "Journey practitioner". I did not know anything about this lady or what she did but I knew it was some sort of spiritual healing and Marley needed a lift in spirit and I thought it might help. The session was really expensive but I told Marley it was a gift from a friend and didn't tell him the amount. He would have never accepted it otherwise. It was a Skype consultation lasting a few hours. He said it was interesting and that she had been very patient going through a lot of emotional issues and that it was worthwhile.

Island retreat

Archie, Annabelle and I went to the airport with him. He had got a remedy to help with some of the symptoms that were returning from our homeopath. Seeing the long queue he would have to stand in with his bags made me worry that he might not have the energy to get on the plane, but thankfully and with huge relief, his Uncle Viliami, who works at the airport, had passed security and went to meet Marley and took him to the plane.

We left the terminal building happy but then I just cried and cried all the way back to the car. I cried tears of pride for his strength, tears of happiness that he was doing something he wanted to do, tears of relief because I was emotionally drained and tears because I missed him already. The kids as usual held me, hugged me and reassured me with positivity. Then I cried tears of pride for Archie and Annabelle being so kind, thoughtful and for making me feel better.

Myself, Annabelle and Archie seeing Marley off at Stansted airport September 2018

Uncle Viliami to the rescue, airside with Marley. Vili sent me this picture and it gave me huge relief to see Marley smiling.

The friend Marley was staying with in Ibiza, secretly sent me photos of him eating his dinner and relaxing to ease my mind, which was so kind of her. His plan was for some space and time to think about what he wanted to do next, maybe go back on the cannabis protocol. He sent me lovely texts and photos most days but after five days said he wanted to come home and go back to square one and that he had stomach aches and a few pains that he had treated with cannabis oil. In his text he apologised for the weeks before he left and said it had been a waste of time. He wanted to focus and do it properly. I felt desperately sorry for him. He had done so well, all alone really in such hard times and he was apologising to me. He was so sweet and I didn't think my heart could break any more, but it did for him that day again at his strength and courage and gentleness.

Marley taking some time to think in Ibiza, September 2018

Marley in Ibiza

Marley came home on the 8th of September. I picked him up early in the morning. He seemed in good spirits and he went straight to bed for a rest. He woke up to a surprise, a little Chihuahua puppy. I had picked him up the day before with my Dad from a massive Traveller site north of Cambridge. I had wanted to get us a puppy for ages thinking it would be good company for Marley, then I changed my mind, thinking it was too much hassle with me working. I didn't want Marley to think of negative connotations, thinking he wasn't going to have a life outside of home. But now taking a break from work and helping Marley get back on track, it seemed the right time. Everyone fell in love with Louis immediately, although Marley was tired and impatient at times with this crazy ball of puppy energy. Louis bought something wonderful into the home. Annabelle was waking up earlier than her alarm to play with him and coming home excited from school, bursting through the door calling his name. Archie had always wanted a puppy so was over the moon. Andy had always wanted a big dog but Louis won him over. Quite unexpectedly he is the best thing in helping our family to heal.

I was pleased for Marley that although he only went to Ibiza for not even a week, he had taken control of his life, booked a ticket and followed through with something he had wanted to do for so long. It was very important for him to do normal things.

His brother Archie had his 22nd birthday and I don't think we did anything special. I apologised to Archie for the lack of birthday cheer. I don't think Archie was particularly bothered, as we were all concerned about Marley.

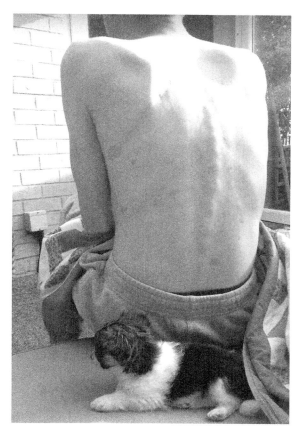

Marley resting with little Louis 9ᵗʰ September 2018

I booked Marley an appointment with a psychotherapist in the following week. She had been recommended to me. Marley had enjoyed the healing session with the spiritual healer before he left for Ibiza. I felt sure that Marley needed to work on his emotions more, and that maybe by understanding them it would help lift his spirits, which is so important in healing cancer or any illness. He enjoyed the session and liked her very much but when he got back in the car he was exhausted and I put it down to him catching up from his trip and not sleeping well. He slept the whole day and that night too.

In the same week, I booked him into hyperbaric oxygen therapy. We had researched it previously when Marley was first diagnosed, but Marley had been unsure at the time. He now wanted to try it as it had been reported to slow down the growth of some cancerous tumours by oxygenating the body. I got back in touch with the integrative cancer charity called Yes to life and they were happy to fund the treatment. It was a bit of a drive and Louis came too. Like most poorly funded treatment centres the place was a bit run down, run by wonderful volunteers who were very kind and friendly. While killing time waiting in the car, I joined the Chrisbeatcancer square one online support group. I wish I had joined it long before as it gave me such a boost. So many people on their cancer journeys. Some who had just been diagnosed, others further on down the line after doing conventional treatment, either fed up of the treatment symptoms and wanting something different or the conventional treatment had not worked for them, and some, like me, caring for a loved one and looking for support and encouragement. What a huge underground movement of such brave people. All trying different things to heal their cancer.

Marley came out after an hour and felt that the oxygen had made him feel more energised but was not a fan of being in a metal tank that looked a bit like a small submarine. He had been shown to a seat, had a mask given to him, then the tank was pressurised. He said he had felt very anxious and had to pace up and down the whole time. So I rang them up to see if there was anything else to be done to relieve him of this claustrophobia. The receptionist was very understanding and said he could sit outside the tank with a mask the following day. He got through the second session but said he didn't want to do any more. That was OK because this was a journey of trial and error. He just was not comfortable there.

If we could have had a tank at home with supervision it would have been better.

On the Saturday after this, a week after his brother's birthday, Marley wanted to take his brother out to lunch at a new pizza place. We had a lovely time, really relaxed and Marley was able to have a vegan pizza and enjoyed it a lot. It felt good for Marley to do something nice for his brother as Archie's birthday had been such a non-event.

Marley, right took Archie out for a belated birthday meal. September 2018

The next day I had booked a spa morning for Andy and I. He was working crazy hours, his back was killing him and he was grumpy, but he was not feeling like it so I took Marley. It was quite nice but busy. We took our lunch in the garden away from everyone and sat with the late September sun toasting our faces. Now that was bliss, quietly together, not saying much, just being, and as Marley often said, we were "Enjoying the silence".

On his return from Ibiza, I had felt Marley becoming increasingly agitated and anxious and we were back to foot rubs and hot water bottles. I booked him another acupuncture session for the Monday. His sleeping was all over the place again and he moved back inside the house on the sofa. I slept on the floor next to him.

Crisis

Tracey from CLIC Sargent came on Tuesday morning and not a moment too soon. I left them to talk, but we were now in crisis. Marley was tired, emotional and having panic attacks. Tracey took command of a sinking ship and after a long time listening to Marley, asked if he would like respite care at the Arthur Rank Hospice, just 15 minutes away. Marley agreed and Tracey told me. I was in total agreement as from previous dealings with the hospice I knew Marley would be in good hands, that the hospice not only deals with "end of life" but could give him a break from us. He would be able to get pain management and his sleep under control and could then set a course of action. Tracey rang them and made all the arrangements. His Dad was not happy and thought Marley would not come out. I really did think my son would be back home after a few days.

After an emotional morning we cancelled the next session with the psychotherapist and Marley rested.

The next day after more broken sleep, Marley had a nice massage. Nicola came to the house as usual. It always made Marley feel good. It took ages for him to get the energy to pack his bag and in the end he gave up and asked if I would do it. He had had a shower then just lay on the landing upstairs. I got him up somehow and into the car.

19th September 2018

We arrived at the Hospice and were shown to inpatients. We were told it was unusually quiet and because of that he could stay for a couple of weeks if he needed it. His room was wonderful, quite big with an ensuite and most importantly a Lazy boy chair. He had patio doors that opened wide with a view of trees and hedges and a couple of bird feeders. He put his bag down and said "I like it here Mum". It was so quiet and tranquil.

On the Thursday I was so tired from so little sleep. My sister Lizzy offered to stay the night with Marley so I could get some rest. I was very relieved when Marley agreed. Lizzy did Reiki with him and sat and talked with him when he couldn't sleep. A different consultant came in each morning, we liked every one of them straightaway. They listened, didn't butt in, and took their time to sort issues and ease Marley's physical symptoms. He turned down morphine, but he agreed on a drug that would stimulate his digestion again as the tumour was stopping the vagus nerve from doing its job. This amazing drug revolutionised Marley's life. His appetite returned and he was so much happier that he could face food again. He was still maintaining a healthy diet , but needed approval from me, so I said at this point he should eat what makes him happy. He ate rounds and rounds of toast and butter. It was quite extraordinary.

A consultant had taken me and Andy aside to say things did not look good. I really can't remember that conversation, only that Andy had stood up and walked out the room.

We went into Cambridge to Jamie's Italian. It was quiet in the afternoon and Marley ordered lots of small dishes and ate slowly, savouring every mouthful. An absolute pleasure to watch.

The red T- shirt 21st September 2018

Marley in the red T-shirt , enjoying the Lazy boy chair

Annabelle and I took Marley out of the hospice to shop. I'd let Annabelle have the day off school. It was important for him to buy a red T-shirt and socks, so off we went. We looked at the Lego Star Wars X wing fighter. Something he had always wanted as a child.

We went back to the Vegan Pizza place as Annabelle had made it quite clear she was not happy that Archie had been taken out without her. I asked the staff to serve us promptly and told them the reason why. Marley ate and was relaxed, then just as I was paying I turned to see shock on his face. I went over and saw that he was upset and panicked after having coughed up blood. Inside I was panicking and thinking "F*CK!" We were nowhere near the taxi rank, in the middle of town on the second floor. How was I going to get him out? Within this brief pause, Marley's expression changed, his face relaxed and he yet again took control. "Mum it's ok, we can walk." I walked in front of him concerned that he may fall down and Annie took the rear. I was still worried until Marley said, "Get a move on Mum, people are trying to get down". We got outside and faced the busy market place. We walked gingerly, seemingly in slow motion as people passed in front of us and across our path. We had got to John Lewis, a cut- through to the car park, when Marley said "F*ck it let's get that red T- shirt, then if I cough up blood again it won't show".

He walked round and round the menswear department. I was still in secret panic mode and had to remember to breathe. Thank God Annabelle was there to help make light of the situation. He chose one at last and we made our way back to the Hospice. That night we all were with him, including Louis who had made a big impression on everyone there, staff and patients alike. I went upstairs to the family room to get some sleep and Annabelle knew I would be worried so sent me a video of Marley sleeping. It was so moving because her sweet little face was in shot with a smile on her face listening to his gentle breathing.

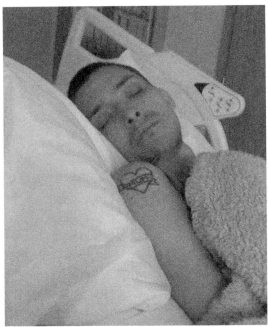

When Marley could sleep soundly, it was a wonderful gift.

Marley's last day on Earth 24th September 2018

I had slept a little before Archie woke me, maybe an hour or so. Marley just wanted me alone and even though I had barely slept, a story from the Bible came to my head when Jesus found his disciples sleeping after he had asked them to stay awake and I thought God will sustain me and give me the energy.

Marley and I talked a lot that night. He asked me questions about my life and family and we went through unfinished business, for hours it seemed. When he got anxious about not sleeping I turned on the lights and said, "well it's almost morning anyway." It was only about 4am, but I didn't tell him that. Marley got on with the Lego his Dad had bought him the day before.

The little cough he had had when we got there five days before had gradually got worse. He was now on oxygen and I felt things were moving fast. I went outside into the corridor and called family and friends to come in to see him. Marley liked the patio doors wide open most of the time and at some point before dawn he went outside and squatted down. I joined him and we looked at the sky together. He was pleased to see his family after breakfast. He was very calm and lost in thought that day and after a lovely visit from his two grandfathers he walked outside and stood looking at the trees for ages on his own. I let him have this time. The pastor, who had visited every day only to be told by Marley he didn't need to see him, came by and I showed him where Marley was. He was not sent away, they stood side by side gently chatting for a long time, looking at the sky and trees, with their backs towards me.

A gentle and steady stream of visitors came throughout the day and Marley was happy to see them, especially Dr Wong. Marley sat on the end of his bed, back straight in the lotus position, so serene and dignified. It was a very emotional meeting to witness, this great doctor saying sincerely and quietly as always that he was so sorry he couldn't help Marley more. Marley thanked him. Marley also spoke of re-educating the dieticians in the cancer clinic and getting rid of the sugary snacks, sweets and drinks in the snack bar in the cancer treatment waiting room. Dr Wong listened carefully and nodded his head. The mood was lightened by the doctor admiring the Star Wars X-Wing fighter still under completion, and with Marley and Archie he discussed favourite characters and spacecraft from the story. Marley and Archie were impressed that Dr Wong's favourite vehicle was an unconventional choice of the Snow speeder.

Marley had a rest and then showed me his bank account on line. The money he had waited for, for such a long time from the Government had at last been transferred. He wanted to take Annie and Archie out shopping. He had a shower that took ages. He was so tired and now the whole family had gathered in the waiting area outside his room around this huge table. Marley smartened himself up and walked slowly out and greeted everyone. He went straight to his Grandma and gave her a kiss. Then said he was tired and went straight back to his bed. He asked me if the doctor could put in a respiratory tube to help his breathing, I told him gently that I didn't think that would be something they could do now.

Last acts of kindness

He told his sister Annabelle that he was sorry but he was too tired to go out, so he made her choose something online. She did then he looked at her choices and said "no not that cheap sh*t, something really nice." Annabelle couldn't decide, so I said to him maybe he should choose and it would be more special. He always had a good eye for gifts. So he did and the effort and determination was unbelievable, as by now the tumour was blocking his windpipe so to take a breath he had to tilt his head back. To order the items on this very computer I am using now, he typed a few words, threw his head back, took a breath, then went back to typing. It took a very long time. He ordered a Ralph Lauren belt for his sister and a Ralph Lauren baseball hat with the year of his birth on it for his brother. It was a pleasure and heart breaking to see him enjoy this arduous task. He wanted to buy Dr Wong a Lego Snow speeder and asked my opinion. He was happy when I totally agreed that it was a wonderful idea.

Marley was concerned that Gracie was not coming to visit until the following week. I told him gently that she was already on a train, on her way from Brighton. More visitors arrived and they were happy to just be there, waiting together. Archie had gone off to get a KitKat for Marley who had accepted that he could now eat whatever he wanted. I had told him to do whatever he wanted to do, eat anything he liked. He wanted ice cream, so Annabelle went off on a mission and came back successful. He said he had forgotten what it tasted like and had another two bowls. His cousin Chae turned up just as Archie was leaving to pick Gracie up from the station. Archie was going to get us all some food. I showed Marley all the messages on Big Love and he was really touched by all the love and prayers. It was hard for him to get comfy but all the nurses were amazing and didn't mind at all to be called back in many times.

Archie and Gracie arrived with what would be his last meal, a very expensive vegan burger. Gracie and I hid ours, we just couldn't eat. Marley was enjoying the company, was relaxed until he started coughing that turned into a bit of a choke. I cleared the room and got a nurse, who gently explained that at this stage sometimes even water can cause choking. The tumour was causing this so she added a thickener that Marley was not interested in swallowing. I could see he was tired. So we put on Blue Planet, a nature documentary, and sent Archie out yet again to buy some Maxibons, his favourite ice-cream. Somehow Blue Planet was playing in Spanish and Marley held up his hands and said "Where is David?" Meaning Sir David Attenborough. We quickly sorted that out and ate our Maxibons, as relaxed as possible.

Marley wanted a rest so we cleared the room again. He wanted me to stay. I tried my best to get him comfortable in the chair, completely surrounded with pillows to keep him upright so he could rest and breathe, but it was near impossible. Looking at him with his chin in his hands, watching as he got more tired. He would relax, then his head would drop which would wake him up again. My heart broke to see him so tired and not able to rest in comfort. He was upset and said he just wanted to sleep. I felt so sorry for him. I remembered his premonition he had told me about some time before when he had shouted in frustration "Don't you realise Mum? I am going to die slowly. I am going to suffocate!" I fetched the nurse, who moved him to the bed and worked on more pillows, but his breathing was now worse so I called Andy, Archie and Annabelle back down from the family room.

Marley died half an hour later. Annabelle sang every song she could think of. We all sang "Three little birds", by Bob Marley and I said prayers out loud. Annabelle and I stood at his feet telling him to go now and be free, with his dad and Archie at his head desperately not wanting him to go. Even in this tragic, most moving experience, stuff happened that we can laugh about now, at ourselves, at our madness. Marley seemed to look up to the ceiling and reached forward with his arms. "Oh my God, he is seeing the light." I said, but then Marley paused and said, "personal space please!" and pushed his arms out to the side. Archie and Andy immediately apologised and let go of their grip. It made me laugh at myself for thinking so stereotypically of death and how people have reported to experience things, when Marley was never stereotypical. At one point Annabelle started singing "My way" by Frank Sinatra. Andy found this too much and started singing "New york, New York" over the top. So looking at my husband and daughter having a sing off, I said, "Stop! Marley do you want Annie to sing?" He nodded and when she then sang "La vie en rose", Marley suddenly sat up, with his eyes still closed, and waved his hands like a conductor in an orchestra. It was beautiful. Then he lay back down.

When he did go, I saw his soul leave his body by the movement in his face and head. I can only describe this moment as like flicking off an old soft woollen sock from a foot. Nearly all the family flooded into the room like a tsunami just moments before he died and we were all together in our raw, almost animalistic grief. Noises came from me that I did not recognise. We all filled that room. Everyone said goodbye to Marley, then moved around holding each other.

After a few hours I put a blanket around me, which dragged on the floor and felt so heavy and walked to the nurses station with Andy, as we had all been left in peace by the staff. I explained to the nurse that we did not know what to do now. She sat us down and explained that we could stay with Marley for as long as we needed and then he would need to be washed and changed into fresh clothes before the undertakers would come and collect Marley's body. I remember telling my family to go home and get some sleep, and when they refused I said that is what Marley would have wanted. He appreciated the need for sleep, so they left. I felt detached from his body and delirious with lack of sleep and shock, so much so that as I climbed the stairs to the family room I didn't know where I was in total confusion. I continued upwards, went through the door and my mind came back. Andy stayed with Marley all through the night and moved his bed so that Marley's face was in the beams of moonlight that were flooding the room. Looking back that gesture to stay with his son all night has meant a lot to me. Knowing his Dad was with him and he was not alone. The staff were supposed to do a changeover with the new team, but they all stayed, and washed and changed him with such care and cried when he was taken out. He was only in the hospice for four days, but his presence made an impact and they still talk about him even now.

I can't place the next few days, but remember going to register his death and that was awful. Sitting in the same, soulless little room where we registered his birth. I sobbed the whole time. The attitude of the reception staff, so cold, so uncaring, put salt in our wounds. Luckily the registrar showed us the respect, acknowledged our pain and made us feel slightly less retched.

October 5th 2018

We have not had the funeral yet, or even decided on what to do with his dear body that served him so well.

When I started this book I had no idea of the ending.

I last worked on it in July and thought it was finished and gave it to Marley to read and I said, "This is your story but written from a mother's perspective. I want you to be honest but be gentle, as it is written from my heart in painful circumstances." He read it and said quietly, "I don't want you to release it. I don't want you to give people false hope". I was confused and thought over night. I ran the next day told my running buddy and she said "But the story, the history remains the same whatever happens". I went back home and explained that to Marley and that I thought it was a book of hope and love.

He said "I think it's a bit boring". That still makes me laugh today, here as I am sitting in Costa, writing and killing time whilst I wait for Annabelle in choir with my life shattered and people getting on with life around me. I will endeavour to make it interesting.

6th November 2018

At Marley's request we went to Granchester Meadows last night. We walked down from the tea rooms towards the river, using our phone torches in the pitch black, moonless night. Crossed a couple of meadows, hoping not to step in cow pats and went through the kissing gates holding Louis . He was whining, I think he was scared of the dark.

We came to the bank where the clairvoyant, (I will explain about her later) had felt the energy to be right.

I had bought a couple of miniature Viking longboats. Andy had made a bamboo raft for them to go on. We also had some floating lanterns and a poster of Marley. It was beautiful but also eerie standing on the bank with the mist rising, the ancient trees silhouetted against the backdrop of distant fireworks and orange glows from bonfires. The river was quite low on the bank and it was not easy for Annabelle to set the boat up on the water and set fire to it. Another comedy of errors as the water was as still as granite so everything just stayed at the edge. Then Annabelle, impatient to launch the poster, let go too early and Marley's face landed face down on the water. We just had to laugh. Then as I walked away I tried to put on some music but couldn't see so gave up, but then one of Marley's favourite pieces just started to play, a breeze came up, took everything downstream gently and it all felt right. I'm glad we made the effort. You see Marley had requested, no, pleaded with me for a funeral pyre whilst in the hospice. It made me laugh at the time as I told him I thought it may be illegal, but he held my hand and looked directly into my eyes and as I paused it was like all the anti-anxiety drug had cleared from his eyes. His pupils dilated and he said, "It's important Mum".

But it was clear from the meeting with our undertakers. (We had researched and got our friend Shirley, a friend on Big Love who is a great researcher and knows a lot about the law, in on the plan. She had spoken to many leaders of different faiths, looked at court cases and we had found private land to build a pyre discreetly and quietly) that they were not prepared to undertake a pyre, possibly damaging their reputation and business. They had already had villagers, concerned about what they had heard, calling them. I was furious. At one point the boss said, knowing our intention, they were well within their rights to not release Marley's body to us. Who knew that our son legally did not belong to us? I just wanted to do what My son had requested so clearly.

My good friend Karen, who had lost her son Joel a few years previously, became my grief coach. She had been to see a spiritualist and had found it healing so I went with Karen to see her as soon as I could. I was feeling stressed by not being able to give my son what he wanted. Even though reeling in raw grief I was still being sensible and was thinking, the energy that we (and everyone who we knew that would jump on board to help us) would use to make this happen, the time it would take, the letters and arguments put forth, the unwanted publicity I decided would be better spent on focussing on getting this book out and carrying out his legacy of changing people's perception of cancer and improving nutrition education in the cancer wards and snack bar. I wanted Marley's legacy to be helping others not, the dead guy who wanted a funeral pyre.

A new experience

We spent two hours with the clairvoyant lady. She didn't charge and never charges apparently for bereaved parents. It was very interesting and many times I felt that Marley was communicating, simply by the words she was using. I was not emotional and quite guarded. At one point she used a crystal pendulum to ask Marley direct questions about his wishes for his body and I got the impression, which was so like Marley, that he was accepting of the current situation of people not being ready for funeral pyres, even though historically, pyres were an acceptable method of disposing of bodies in this country. At the end of two hours I felt happy that decisions were made and I could get on with it. Marley communicated that he did not like being in the chapel of rest, he wanted to be outside with the sun shining on his grave, in the middle of the glade and not in the shade of any trees. He said he was content and wanted to express how much bigger the afterlife was, more than we ever thought it would be, but he was not happy that his request for a funeral pyre was causing me stress, so basically get on with it. He gave instructions for the symbolic Viking longboat pyre, on fireworks night, as there would be distractions and people would not bother us on our mission. It had to be made from biodegradable materials and on a point of the river that was quieter at Granchester Meadows. The clairvoyant couldn't quite pinpoint the location as it was not familiar to her. After a while of her struggling I said "Near the tearooms?" and she laughed and agreed as she felt a huge gust of cold air or energy. This made total sense as the tearooms is my favourite place on earth. He communicated *"bury my body in the woodland burial ground but think of me when you visit Granchester"*. As soon as

I got home I made a pendulum and although I could move it a tiny bit with a slight movement, it is impossible to get a pendulum to stop instantly like it had done on request in that little room. I was content that what I had witnessed had been legitimate and real.

We had gone with family members to visit Marley at the chapel of rest several times. The last time we saw him Annabelle wanted to place a letter in his pocket from her. She was eager to see him and I wanted her to hang back because I did not know if nature had changed his features in death. She didn't heed my warning and went in first and was devastated to see the difference. I felt so sorry for her.

Marley's burial was pretty perfect really. Slightly unconventional and beautiful. In the morning we all had breakfast together. We also had two of Marley's good friends staying, which was lovely, and the company of those who loved him was a huge comfort. My oldest friend Sue flew in from Ireland and was a great support. As we were getting ready, someone noticed an amazing rainbow in the sky and as we all went out into the garden to see the colours grew more intense. It lasted for ages in strong colour. Big Love were sending me pictures from their perspective in the surrounding villages. There was no rain to be seen anywhere, very peculiar, extraordinary and we accepted it was a gift from Marley. We were strangely relaxed and content.

The extraordinary rainbow that so many witnessed on the morning of Marley's burial.

We walked behind the hearse, forming a big procession. It was not a short walk and I was grateful of that last walk with our boy.

Marley was not in a casket; he was wrapped in a shroud, then in his grandmother's patchwork quilt, sort of Native American Indian style. I don't think the undertakers had dealt with this sort of arrangement before and I felt that Andy going over to support them in positioning his body for the ceremony had been a very good idea. Andy had spent the afternoon previously hand making the board that Marley would be placed on to be lowered into the grave. We did laugh quietly when a gust of wind lifted the blanket nearly off. I was thinking Marley was up to mischief again!

I was touched that our former Reverend Jessica, now a Canon came, together with our current Reverend, Petra, to do the service together. Without a casket, the bit where they lay their hands on Marley to commit his body meant so much more when they actually laid their hands on him. They took turns in saying prayers and it was quite beautiful. The sun shone on Marley the whole time. He was laid in the grave. Andy, had had the presence of mind to cut huge fronds from our palm tree that Marley had looked at for hours in his last summer. He gave us each one to lay on his body, starting at his head, I was glad that they would protect his face from the earth. Then we threw in sprigs of rosemary (Marley's favourite herb), and red leaves from another tree that grows in our garden. His best friend laid a pack of cards, a great pastime of theirs and another a set of headphones. I started singing "Three little birds" by Bob Marley, and everyone who knew it joined in. After a while I walked back to the burial ground lodge with the Canon and the Reverend, who I also class as good friends. They were visibly moved by the ceremony. I turned and said; "I feel Ok, I feel content" and Canon Jessica said, "You are being sustained". I felt it, all the love.

The sun shining on us all at the woodland burial ground.

After everyone had left, Andy, Archie, Marley's male cousins and friends wanted to put the earth on Marley themselves. Another gesture from his father that meant so much to me and I was reassured that he was laid to rest with love and care.

At the same time as the burial in Barton, in our village the bell ringers rang a quarter peel for Marley. A friend recorded them. Such kindness.

Two days later the service was held at our church. Poster-sized pictures of Marley's life were hung. Beautiful flowers had been arranged by another friend to include sunflowers and carrots of course. His sister, Annabelle, sang beautifully from her soul, even after her backing track cut out whilst singing 'Time after time' she carried on, her voice carrying into the eaves and echoing amongst the silent congregation that were in awe. We felt Marley had interfered with it. She didn't need the backing track anyway. She sang 'La vie en rose' at the end, which she sang to Marley just before he died. Everyone who attended will never forget her singing.

We had a full choir, all of whom were in tears most of the time along with everyone else. I stared down at Marley's beautiful service sheet that another friend had hand-painted and thought of the many people who had supported us on this journey.

A beautiful service with many people travelling from far and wide.

Andy and I spoke separately, side by side, from the heart. It was incredibly difficult and took lots of pauses to compose ourselves, but I was determined for people to know about Marley's life.

Tracey from CLIC Sargent also spoke about Marley's last year. The Sermon from the Reverand was also extraordinary, so much so you could have heard a pin drop. I think that she may have converted a few sitting on the fence about Christianity in that packed church.

When the service ended we listened to "Be thankful for what you got", by William DeVaughn and everyone just stayed in their seats. No one seemed to want to leave the church or that song. It was beautiful.

The funeral wake was also perfect and sorted by another friend. I wanted to provide food that Marley would have liked. Vats of spiced daal, curry and accompaniments, a tea bar and no alcohol. Marley never drank, so in respect to him I made that call. The whole community, led by my sister Sarah, provided healthy cakes that Marley would have approved of. When we walked into the hall, I felt humbled, as I looked at all the serving stations and I saw it was all my dear friends from our village serving everyone else. That meant such a lot to us.

Throughout the whole of that last year we were sustained by our family and friends. They carried us.

Chapter Two - Marley's Protocols

I am not a doctor or scientist. I found the biology and some medical terms and names tricky and sometimes it made my eyes glaze over, even when Marley was reading stuff out. I have learnt a great deal though.

Do not be afraid.

I will go on about Chris Wark a lot. He has survived cancer and had dedicated his life to helping other people. I re-read his book again as my editor suggested, expanding information on the protocols, whereas I was hoping to (lazily) just direct people to Chris Wark. To be honest I work full time and I don't have time to expand further. Other people have done that already. Finding what works best for you can be simple or you can make research a life-changer. I already have a day-job and I personally, preferred to watch the YouTube videos.

Chris has studied more than any other professor on the subject. He is right in saying in his book that some people make the mistake of putting the healing down to one thing, for example, no sugar or just high-fibre diets. I have learnt you have to adapt and change and follow your instinct on much of the research. So the following is a mash-up of Chris Wark's findings with Dr. Xandria Williams and other research we Googled. Marley was very serious about his healing and would only look at something if it had science based evidence. I was given permission from Chris Wark to use his research and findings in this book.

Chris Wark put together a set of video-teaching modules called 'The Square One Healing Cancer Coaching Program', covering every aspect of healing. You may choose another cancer coach, but what is essential is that all aspects need to be looked at, not just nutrition, not just supplements or the spiritual side. Jump in and cover all of them and if you join the Square One support group there are over 12,000 other healers/carers to support you. I am still on there and feel a bit of a fraud now, but sometimes I send a message to someone having a bad day or to the family who have lost someone through cancer. It's hard, reading their posts after following their story, but then you get a post of someone having a clear PET scan and it is wonderful.

A quick note of what is in Chris Wark's modules

1.The first module is free and is important because you learn about cancer and how to overcome fear and discouragement; the 'Beat cancer mindset' that every successful survivor has in common; the importance of a support system and how to enjoy life and your healing journey.

Eliminating fear was very liberating for me as Marley's carer and gave me 100% confidence in his choice.

2. Possible causes of why you have cancer and how to remove them from your life. Lessons from countries around the world with the lowest cancer rates.

3 and 4. The anti -cancer diet. A comprehensive guide, backed with science. A daily schedule to follow, including juicing and recipes.

5. How to detox your body and environment. How you can improve and accelerate the process. As well as using juicing, drinking more water, (we bought a stainless steel gravity water purifier and he drank from PBA free bottles), supplements to stimulate his liver, green tea, exercising and enemas, Marley changed all of his skin

and hair-care products to natural non-toxic ones including his toothpaste and washing detergent. He stopped using deodorant and just washed throughout the day if need be.

6. Learn about, and eliminate stress, learn about the power of your thoughts, how to overcome fear and anxiety.

Marley used acupuncture, reflexology, yoga, meditation, reiki healing. His change of nutrition and lifestyle definitely made a difference.

I also want to include a tool he was give by the psychotherapist he went to see. It really helped Marley and may help any of you at some point. It is called Coping breathing space and is on the next page.

Coping breathing space

***Stage 1**. Acknowledging awareness of the difficulty.*

Bring yourself into the present moment by deliberately adopting an erect and dignified posture. If possible close your eyes. Ask yourself:

"What is going on with me at the moment?
"What is my experience in my thoughts, my
feelings, my bodily sensations?"

Stage 2. *Gathering, redirecting attention.*

Gentle redirect and focus your full attention
into the breathing. Follow the breath all the
way in and all the way out.

The breath functions as an anchor bringing
you into the present helping you to tune into
a state of awareness and stillness. Allow the
out-breath to ease away the more
unpleasant experiences.

Stage 3. *Expanding awareness and*
attention.

Allow your awareness to gently encompass
the whole body, the space it takes up, as if
your whole body is breathing.

Include any sense of discomfort, tension or
resistance.

Have a sense of the space around you, hold
everything with a softening and opening. As
best you can bring this expanded awareness
to the next moments of your day.

I found it useful in the following year, when experiencing panic attacks, to remind myself that I have been through this before and can get through it again.

I stop and slow my breathing down.

Back to the modules….

7. The importance of spiritual healing.

Marley was not religious and did not attend church, but he respected my beliefs and felt honoured when asked to be Annabelle's Godfather and took his role very seriously. He did feel that there was something special in this world that he could not explain.

Marley worked on his spirituality and explored different things. He had long discussions with his Grandma and read quite a bit on the subject. He turned his life around. Some people may never address this in their life. Marley was forced to and became a happier person, forgiving and accepting.

8. The importance of exercise, rest and sleep.

Marley used the trampoline every day, did yoga, went to CrossFit, slept when tired and used supplements, massage and acupuncture, to improve his sleep patterns. A lot of healing happens during sleep. When Marley first came home his sleep pattern was completely messed up. It didn't take long after the operation and implementing his protocols to turn it around. As I say to all the very tired new parents I work with, sleep deprivation is used in many parts of the world as a torture because it is very effective at breaking a person's spirit.

9. **Cancer healing herbs, teas and supplements.**

You will learn about all of the above and how they support the body's ability to repair, regenerate and detoxify. There are five supplement categories covered.

Nutritional support

Immune support

Anti-cancer

Anti-virus/bacterial/parasite

Detoxification.

10. **How to test and monitor your progress.**

This module will give you the proper prospective and what to expect as you go along in your healing journey. The benefits and side effects of all the different diagnostic machines. Also information on blood markers and what you should be watching out for.

We were lucky to have a great doctor. He accepted and respected Marley's choice and when we asked if he would monitor Marley's progress, he agreed without hesitation. So Marley chose repeat CT scans.

Marley's way

The first thing Marley did immediately whilst still in hospital was cut out all sugar, to stop feeding the cancer. He didn't eat a lot of processed sugar but there are sugars in bread, pasta, fruits. The best I could do while he was in hospital was to bring him cold-pressed vegetable juices. The ones I had been buying were pasteurised and so some of the nutrients had been destroyed in the process.

He replaced wheat bread with organic sunflower bread, which when toasted, is delicious.

Fruits are very important too, so Marley had, raspberries, blueberries, strawberries and sometimes bananas. Eaten together it slows down the release of fruit sugars in the banana.

He ate organic vegetables. If you can't get or afford organic veggies any will do, just wash them thoroughly. Forget one of your five a day. Think 80% of your diet.

Marley cut out all processed foods. Cook from scratch as you know then what you are eating. Very occasionally we would go out to waggamama or a vegan café. He would eat organic fruit and nut bars as a treat.

Marley cut out caffeine, alcohol, and meat. He got protein from nuts, seeds and pulses like beans and lentils. He cut out all dairy except a small amount of hard goats cheese, replaced cows milk with unroasted almond milk or coconut milk.

Marley was eating eggs, but stopped 6 months post-op.

He drank a lot of organic green tea and water with lime throughout the day.

Marley's Juice (all organic if possible)

Juicing is the best way to extract massive amounts of nutrients from vegetables. Juicing releases approximately 90% of the nutrients in food and these are rapidly absorbed in the digestive process.

6 carrots. (rich in vitamins, minerals, flavonoids, carotenoids. They are a good natural source of sodium, potassium, calcium, magnesium, iron, phosphorus, sulphur, silicone and chlorine.) Some people worry about the sugar content in carrots but in the case of juicing, nutrients that can turn off cancer genes, interfere with cancer cell reproduction and cause apoptosis, (cancer cell suicide) sort of overrides that.

1 apple (have a prebiotic effect and promote good gut bacteria)

6 sticks of celery (antioxidant, reduces inflammation, supports digestion, rich in vitamins and minerals. Has an alkalizing effect.)

1/3 cucumber (antioxidant, high in vitamins and minerals)

A big piece of fresh ginger. (contains anti cancer properties).

A handful of Kale (nutrient powerhouse, antioxidant and **one handful of spinach**, (calcium rich, vitamins, minerals, folic acid), but you can put that straight in the blender if you wish.

He added this to the blender with a cup of blueberries and a whole lemon. (with rind cut off) Sometimes raspberries and a banana.

To this he added supplement powders that we got from Dr Williams and Amazon.

A spoonful of Pure Synergy berry powder

The organic berry powder is a phytonutrient and antioxidant.

A scoop of IP6 in Inositol

IP6 is found in beans, nuts, seeds, rice and wheat bran, corn and sesame. It is composed of an inositol sugar molecule (one of the B vitamins). It normalises the rate of cell growth. IP6 repairs the gene mutations and re-establishes control within the cells, their rate of division is slowed.

IP6 has been documented to increase natural killer cells which are white blood cells that help protect against infection or cancerous cells.

IP6 inhibits cancer cell migration and invasion. It also helps to stop inflammation. It is also an antioxidant, known to protect against disease. IP6 is significantly more potent than green tea.

A teaspoon of Radiance C

Vitamin C supports nearly every system in your body and it neutralises free radicals. The sicker or more toxic you are, the more free radicals you have in your body, and as a result, the more vitamin C your body will absorb and use.

Lecithin granules

A source of essential fatty acids and nutrients that support cell and mitochondrial membranes, and brain and liver function.

A dessert spoon of Pure Synergy Green powder.

A superfood of vitamins, minerals, enzymes, fibre and special nutrients like chlorophyll. Natural antioxidant.

He also took as supplements

Turmeric/curcumin. 6 per day

Research has found curcumin (an Indian spice) reduces the spread of cancer cells and potentially increases the effectiveness of chemotherapy. It kills cancer cells and prevents more from growing. Marley's supplement contained black pepper to increase the curcumin absorption.

Vitamin D

In 2016, a landmark study published in PLOS ONE journal, found that women over 55 with blood concentrations of vitamin D higher than 40ng/ml, had a **67% lower risk** of cancer compared to women with levels lower than 20ng/ml. The researchers concluded that optimal levels for cancer prevention are between 40 and 60ng/ml, and most cancers occur in people with vitamin D blood levels of between 10 and 40ng/ml. Most experts agree that the best source of vitamin D is sunshine, which is good advice but depends on multiple factors, your age, your BMI, your skin tone, your distance from the equator, the season and the weather. If it's cloudy or smoggy, that can block out as much as 60% of D3 producing UV rays from the sun.

So maybe get tested and monitor.

Magnesium is also critical for D3 absorption. Magnesium deficiency shuts down the vitamin D synthesis and metabolism pathway.

I used to suffer from insomnia and "runners legs". I would lay down feeling tired then my legs would spasm and I had this intense feeling that I wanted to go for a run and it was only alleviated by stretching repeatedly. My Mum suggested taking magnesium/calcium supplements. Some supplements take a while to kick in but I had a great nights sleep almost from week one. I use one earplug now and if I do wake I use Rescue Remedy Night Tincture, made by

Bach flower remedies and I go straight back to sleep.

Liver support 6 per day

A multi-vitamin for Marley's metabolic type from a nutritionalist. Supports the liver to work super efficiently helps to detox the body, and helps to get rid of any nasties quicker.

Apricot kernels B17/ Laetrile

We found these very interesting, we did not know there was a kernel inside the pit. Rich in vitamin E, an antioxidant and they contain amygdalin. When someone eats amygdalin, it converts to cyanide in the body. It can be lethal. I ate six in one go as they are quite Moreish and got a piercing headache, **as a warning not to mess with the kernels**. Research the doses and start with a low amount and build up. A controversial natural cancer-fighting substance but many cancer healers think of it as a natural chemo. It is very cheap to buy, banned in parts of USA.

Water

Water is of paramount importance in assisting our ability to detoxify.

Marley drank plenty of filtered water with cut limes in it as limes have an alkaline effect on the body.

Cancer thrives in an acidic environment. He tested his alkalinity with strips that he peed on. The vegetable juices, cutting sugar out and plenty of water help to reduce the Acidity.

Cancer also thrives in an oxygen depleted environment so Marley tried to get as much oxygen to his cells by exercise and he used the "Budwig" protocol.

Johanna Budwig was a German biochemist. She found in her research that oils high in omega 3s mixed with a sulphuric protein like cottage cheese or sheep's yoghurt would bring oxygen straight to the cells. Cancer, being an anaerobic-functioning cell does not like oxygen. It does not function with it. Cancer cells get their energy from glucose. Hence Marley's desire to get sugar snacks out of the oncology departments in hospitals.

Marley used sheep's yoghurt (protein) with natural, organic flaxseed oil. Blend for one minute then let it stand for 10 minutes. He chopped almonds, walnuts and sunflower seeds and put them on top. You can add berries or berry powder to hide the taste. It can have a very strong taste and you have to make it palatable.

He replaced yoghurt with organic hemp protein powder after five months.

Marley's daily diet

We found it really useful to write everything down on a daily spread sheet or table, showing food, supplements, exercise and how the day went, emotionally and energy-wise. He tried to eat as much raw food as possible with the majority being vegetables. Herbs and spices are very beneficial so Marley would use them all the time. Rosemary, basil, ginger, oregano, sage and thyme and a lot of garlic.

Marley started the day always with **green tea**

First juice then.

Breakfast

Eggs and avocado on organic sunflower-seed bread or oats with almond milk, berries and nuts.

Lunch

Avocado, garlic and a squeeze of lemon squashed onto sunflower bread, (gluten-free), or organic soup.

Or a rainbow salad with leaves, mixed peppers, onion, tomatoes, cucumber, avocado.

Marley loved snacks, homemade hummus and corn crackers or gluten free oat crackers. Nuts and seeds. Plain popcorn with a bit of cinnamon. Rice crackers. All organic.

Aubergine and tomato with chickpea pasta.

Second juice

Evening Dinner

Curry made with different beans, chickpeas and veg.

Gluten-free wrap stuffed with salad.

Organic vegetarian soups and gluten-free bread.

Eggs on avocado

Gluten-free pasta with homemade organic sauces.

Gluten-free falafels.

There are many good ideas and suggestions for recipes on the internet, to make the meals interesting and varied. I have just given you a few of Marley's favourites.

Marley's daily routine/ lifestyle, after recovering so quickly from major surgery

Make juice

Yoga session in his room. He went to a few classes then did it at home.

Boot-camp session at Bearwalden CrossFit gym.

Breakfast

Research

Budwig protocol

Chores or meet with a CLIC Sargent volunteer

Lunch

Research, relaxing

Dinner

Visit friends, or they would come over.

When he started the cannabis protocol Marley would get everything done then take it in the afternoon as it would make him very relaxed.

Words to lift the spirit

I have included quotes that I found lifted my spirits, (from people that you will recognise and from people and organisations that may be new to you, and some I really don't know where they came from.) To comfort and reassure on those really bad days when dark sunglasses aren't dark enough! Sometimes I just Googled "Quotes to give hope", or "quotes for courage".

The Lord's Prayer.

My Mum says, "sometimes there is nothing you can do but cling hold of one another and pray". I did that a lot with my mum.

Sometimes the future can seem overwhelming so take it a day a time and if necessary take it half-hourly or even minute by minute and appreciate the minutes you get through. From the Al-Anon book "Courage to Change"

"Everything I need is always provided"

"I am always in the right place at the right time"

"I am [or the name of your loved one] always divinely protected and guided."

"I trust in the process of life"

All affirmations from Louise Hay "You can heal your life"

"Cross each bridge when you come to it."

"Miracle follows miracle and wonders never cease"

"God will only give you as much as you can take."

"We must accept infinite disappointment, but never lose infinite hope."

Martin Luther King Jr

"Hope is being able to see that there is light despite all of the darkness" *Desmond Tutu*

"You may not always have a comfortable life and you will not always be able to solve all of the world's problems at once but don't ever underestimate the importance you can have because history has shown us that courage can be contagious and hope can take on a life of its own" Michelle Obama

"The journey of a thousand miles begins with one step" *Lao Tze*

"With the new day comes new strength and new thoughts" *Eleanor Roosevelt*

Calm mind brings inner strength and self-confidence, so that's very important for good health" *Dalai Lama*

"No one saves us but ourselves. No one can and no one may. We ourselves must walk the path" *Buddha*

"A hero is an ordinary individual who finds the strength to persevere and endure in spite of overwhelming obstacles" *Christopher Reeve*

"When adversity strikes, that's when you have to be the most calm. Take a step back, stay strong, stay grounded and press on". *LL Cool J, an American rapper*

My Grandfather once said: "The best sermon is from one's life, not from ones lips", so I try and live true to his words and to the prayer below and I find it helps.

Just for today I will try and live through this day only and not tackle all my problems at once.

I will choose to be happy.

I will adjust myself to what is, and not try to adjust everything to my own desires.

I will try to strengthen my mind. I will study and will learn something useful. I will read something that requires effort, thought and concentration.

I will exercise my soul in three ways. I will do someone a good turn and not be found out. I will do at least 2 things that I don't want to just for exercise.

I will not show anyone that my feelings are hurt, they may be hurt but today I will not show it.

I will be agreeable, I will look as well as I can. Dress becomingly, keep my voice low, be courteous, criticise not one bit. I won't find fault with anything, nor try to regulate or improve anyone but myself.

I will have a programme. I may not follow it exactly, but I will save myself from two pests. Hurry and indecision.

I will have a quiet half hour to reflect and get a better perspective of my life.

I will not be afraid.

Al-Anon.

Lord make me an instrument of thy peace. Where there is hatred, let me sow love.

Where there is injury, pardon; where there is doubt, faith; where there is despair, hope; where there is darkness, light and where there is sadness, joy.

Believe you me, It's hard some days to carry this all out and some days I want to smash stuff. I do the best I can.

Resources I found really helpful

Chrisbeatcancer.com

Chris Wark was diagnosed in 2002, with stage 3 colon cancer. He had surgery but refused Chemo and radiation treatment. He is a realtor in America, has a wife and two children. After 7 years of being cancer-free he went public. He has done so much research. He is an author, speaker and health coach and has been on talk shows.

You can see survival stories, resources and great info on his website.

Chris also has a cancer-coaching programme called The Square One modules. It does cost money but worth every penny and sometimes he does a deal so it is half price. With the membership you get free access to the square 1 support group that is invaluable.

"The Truth about Cancer" By Ty Bollinger (Love his name)

Ty has his own website, Documentary series, books, YouTube videos.

The Cancer Revolution

Integrative Medicine

The future of cancer care

"Your guide to integrating complementary and conventional medicine."

By Patricia Peat

This amazing book came to be unexpectedly from my cousin who I rarely see. It was dropped into me one day (another little miracle) and when I started reading I couldn't stop. The book is full of information from a world-class team of experts. It also has 40 pages of websites and further reading.

CLIC Sargent

A charity to support children up to the age of 25 years diagnosed with cancer and a support for families too.

www://togetheragainstcancer.org.uk

yestolife.org.uk

Yes to Life aims to empower people with cancer to make informed decisions about their cancer care options. It provide information to guide people through the confusing options for care and lifestyle choices.

The China Study

By T.Colin Campbell

A 20 year study and one of the best selling books on nutrition. The study examines the link between the consumption of animal products (including dairy) and chronic illnesses such as heart disease, diabetes and cancer.

Stupidcancer.org (American but great web page with loads of information)

A non-profit organization to help young adults with cancer.

Internet searches...As said before, I know a lot of us do this and there is some great stuff on there but with all research information these people give you, look at testimonials. I preferred to go with Chrisbeatcancer because he researched so many of these sites and would only put links on his site of ones he thought were legit. There are some interesting people out there!!

Chapter Three: My background and why it is easy to support my son in his decision.

Before my grandfather died we had formed a great relationship and I had tried to take down his history to keep. We only got as far as his early years (he had an interesting life). He was born in India in 1916 and, as was traditional then, was shipped back to England for schooling when he was 10, with his siblings. His parents returned to India but his mother would send him parcels containing homeopathic remedies for coughs, colds and other common ailments. Apparently this was quite common. Many years ago, my grandfather while in Cambridge, sat with others around a kitchen table forming the Organic Soil Association. He always had an allotment and learnt a lot about food production when forced to be a farmer during the war. He found it very difficult to get work as a teacher as he was a conscientious objector. So you can see my family is not afraid to go against the grain.

When I was a child, we would have cod liver oil every day and brewer's yeast (Vit

B) and Vitamin C. We had fresh vegetables from the garden and little sugar. Later on when my Mum left my Dad she developed an early onset of crippling arthritis in her hips. She went to a naturopathic doctor and went on a full raw-food diet, no fish, no fowl and it alleviated the pain. I remember mum read Adelle Davis "Let's get well ". Mum was broke so meals were mostly vegetarian and homemade. As teenagers we had homemade muesli for breakfast, went to school with homemade coleslaw, sesame-seed crackers, homemade lemonade. I can't say I loved it but I hardly ever got spots and was hardly ever at the doctors. When I was 16 my friends thought it was hilarious to buy me a bag of bird's seed for my birthday present! So keeping healthy, vitamin supplements and homemade, healthy food was part of my upbringing.

When Marley was born, he was breastfed for six months. In hindsight I wish I had had the confidence to carry on longer, but breast feeding can be so frustrating sometimes as well as a joy, and I wish Mother Nature could have put a visible gauge somewhere of how much Marley was drinking to reassure me he was getting enough food.

At six weeks old a cold went to his chest which led to bronchiolitis and his lungs collapsed. After recovering from that awful illness, he developed childhood asthma and every cold he got went straight to his chest. I am ashamed of his early diet. He was quite fussy and even though my mum would advise otherwise, I gave him what he would eat. If I could go back I would wean him a lot better on steamed broccoli and cauliflower florets and other veg when he was hungry then give him protein and carbohydrates after. I have learnt so much about nutrition over the years and his younger sister had a much healthier diet after being breastfed for a year and a half and weaned on better food.

The children in my care, I am happy to report, have brilliant packed lunches and dinners, full of vegetables, fish, fruit, nuts and seeds. Water at the ready, no more fruit juice or squash laden with sugar and preservatives. The recommended amount of exercise for a toddler used to be 30 minutes a day. Now it is three hours. We enjoy outdoor activity every day, whatever the weather, as long as you have the right clothing there is no such thing as bad weather and the children are happier for it and much more focussed when we start other, quiet activities. When I take the kids out for outdoor learning in the forest or park, it always surprises me how agile and strong they are. All kids like to climb and hang it seems.

Diet, education and research has come a long way. Better outcomes start with better nutrition and exercise as infants. It is leading back in a big circle back to how it used to be before mass food production.

The people we have loved and lost

Johnie

When I was three or four years old my Uncle Johnie came to live with us. I remember liking him very much. He was a lot younger than my mum. I think he was being a pain at home. He was only 16 and the great-fun sort of uncle that throws you up in the air and plays chase. He loved football and wore cool, great 70's flares. He was diagnosed with leukaemia whilst living with us. I remember going to visit him in Hammersmith Hospital and it being next to a prison.

He was cared for by a lovely Indian nurse called Barbie. She came to stay with us for a while, and I remember her in the kitchen making chapattis, which is not really the norm in a farmhouse kitchen in South Cambridgeshire. I still keep in touch with Barbie and rang her after Marley's diagnosis to get her advice.

I remember going into his hospital room with my mum, he was in a special see-through tent to protect him from germs. There were space suit-like gloves attached to the tent. Johnie sat up on his bed with a beaming smile, so happy to see me, stretched out his hand I think through the glove, but he had lost a lot of hair and weight and didn't look like Johnie. I remember seeking refuge behind mum. I didn't take his hand and I knew he was disappointed as my mum was explaining my shyness. I still feel bad about that today. I know it's a ridiculous feeling as I was so young and my behaviour completely understandable, but I still feel it.

My Grannie used to stay the week with him, leaving my aunts at home in Birmingham, and then change over with my Grandad at the weekend. My grandparents had to make the decision to turn off his life support. Even though they have both died now my heart goes out to them.

Johnie went to Hammersmith Hospital in December 1973 and died in the April 1974. The chemo he was on was experimental. Childhood leukaemia is one of the cancers that chemo has increased the survival rates for over the years, so our Johnie helped. X

Recently my Mum showed up with this letter she wrote to her brother Johnie five years after he passed away. I am including it to show thankfully, that things have improved in cancer care, as in the bedside manner of doctors for a start. She said she was just so angry after he died, but with us four kids to look after and a broken marriage to sort out she buried it all until one morning she just woke up and wrote the following text in one go, without a pause. She wrote:

Do they ever know what to say, those white coated men?
Can anything prepare us for what will come?
So we took you there. Acute they said.
We sat and waited while they tested you.
X-rays, spinal injections.
And then in capacious overalls we were let in, scrubbed clean.
The anemia unit they called it.
Mummy came from Birmingham to be with you.
And home we went uncertain.
You looked the same, paleish and horribly clean.
A month passed, we chatted on the phone.
They sent you home for Christmas, lucky you until Bulsulfan started working.
You were frightened then and glad to return to the white coated men.

An isolation tent became your home, a plastic bubble.

And we couldn't touch you any more when we reached out to hold your hand we met plastic.

The "side effects" began.

Oh! They told us, you were a guinea pig, they told us they didn't know what would happen. Well we found out.

Your hair fell out, your mouth was blue. Violet from the gentian violet for the mouth ulcers.

The burn marks on your body.

You couldn't swallow, could you? And yet they gave you whole pills to swallow.

You didn't feel like eating, who could blame you. Swallowing wasn't easy. We stirred.

We began to go to war for you.

We suggested that instead of sterile pre-packed food, tins of Heinz baby foods would do.

Fruit dessert, cool refreshing, you liked that.

You began to pick up again.

Another month passed.

I bought you in some snowdrops, against the rules of course.

I sealed them outside, so they were sterile.

At least you saw them. A little of the countryside you loved.

And the cards come. I wonder if the nurses remember your room.

The rest were spotless and cold, but yours was full of love.

Papa wrote you didn't he?

Everyday you had a card, everyday something to help you.

The nurses read them too.

I read them then went to the rest room to cry.

Where did he get such strength and love from?

At weekends Mummy went home and papa came to you.

They didn't see much of each other.

There was a crisis, your tube was knocked out. Panic. Bunches of white coated men flocked in and out.

They learnt to crush your pills so you could swallow them.

Mummy said prayers for all of you, with you.

Raj died. He pulled his tubes out. He wanted death.

Time came, we dreaded.

They replaced our frozen bone marrow.

We waited to see if it would take.

I remember you crying, down the phone, I remember it well.

"It's gone acute again" you said.

My red hot car, my Citroen, how we moved down the A1 to support Mummy.

The second try, the same dose of Bulsulphan.

5 gms they said.

The white coats flocked in, flocked out. No choice.

A week passed.

The flawless daffodil bulbs faded.

How you bled, no lining left in your throat this time.

They pumped blood in

You pumped it out.

I couldn't eat my supper.

I cried at home

I sat in the passage between the children's room for prayer and cried at it all.

Drugs helped

Fortral they gave you.

Within a week you begged for it.

They gave you water you were calmed.

A drug addict.

I came and went three times a week

We all had tests for our white cells.

We took our turns upstairs

The centrifuge machine

I carried down the little bag

Seven hours to achieve so little

They gave it to you straight away

I saw it drip into you

My cells might help you

Mummy's might

At least we did something to help.

You began to strengthen again.

We waited.

We prayed.

Father Whelan wrote

He likened Mummy to Mary at the foot of the cross.

She slept on a camp bed in your room, the hospital made an exception.

You were so young at 16.

You asked Mummy once, "How does it feel to die?"

"Like falling asleep" She said and cried in her bed of hopelessness.

The white coated men coughed.

More tests,

You sat on the pot near the plastic and I rubbed your back.

We read you stories of the Vet and laughed together.

You never complained

You were so thin and bald

You wouldn't wear your wig for me

And then we learnt Acute again, Blast cells are back.

You were much weaker then

You couldn't sit in bed.

I cried reading Palm Sunday Gospel

Maggie said

"Papa feels that treatment must stop"

They could have kept you alive they said, with all their modern aids for about 6 months

What for, in a bubble?

Poor papa, He begged them to release you, to stop treatment.

Into the barrier nursing room they took you out of the bubble.
With no treatment 24 hours they said
Next day we made arrangements
Robin drove me up
Papa went for a rest, you'd of thanked him in the morning.
You seemed asleep
And I could touch you, warm flesh, no plastic, no drips.
Mummy was at Weston that weekend, for a break.
I got there at 12
I sat with you
Moments passed
You stirred and opened your eyes and shut them again
Every time someone came I told you
Moments passed each time and then you opened your eyes as if to greet them.
Robin would not wait And you sat up for him but he had gone
To cry alone and missed your effort
I cried silently
I knew you loved him
We sat around your bed
At 3 o' clock I read the Palm Sunday Gospel to you
You slept through that
Maggie came
Mummy came and cried and cried
So tired, so tired

She was grey and beaten
Supper time came, I wouldn't go
It rang in my ears
"Can you not watch with me one hour?"
"Yes Johnie you shall not die alone"
We rang everyone to pray
I sat silent by you, holding your hand
That lovely nurse, she was new that day, stayed with me
I was afraid
She felt your pulse, not long she said
Not long she said again
I feared they would not come back in time
The pulse was faint when they came in
Mummy began to pray out loud
We all did
That awful pause
A breath, another pause
Then a silence began
"He's gone" the nurse said
"Out of the depths"…Began my crying mother
We all cried
Maggie climbed up to kiss you
"He gave us so much" she said
"Dear God, Thank you" I said
"Thank you for giving him peace"
Father Foster came in and blessed you
We waited for Greg to arrive, I took him to you and we went home. Four months of being a modern martyr.

I think this is a very beautiful piece of writing. One of the many reasons my mum makes me so proud to be her daughter.

Jobug

When Marley was nine years old I was pregnant with my daughter and really sick in bed with morning sickness. Jobug, a friend of a friend, came to visit me. She had just started radiotherapy and was feeling dreadful. She laid on the bed with me, both of us feeling shitty. She tried my travel bands on, which had alleviated some of my sickness, and as we lay in misery we bonded. So she was not a childhood best friend, she was really in my life for about a year and a half and I had the privilege to walk alongside her during that last bit of her journey in this life. She had been diagnosed with skin cancer after a dentist spotted something on the roof of her mouth. Her mother had died of cancer at 35 and Jobug was 35 too when she died, but not before chemo, radiotherapy and a trip to Germany, which I presume was a Gerson therapy treatment centre. She was told that she would never be able to have children but she turned it around and she wanted to train to become a clown and volunteer in children's wards. Jobug the clown, one of life's cheerleaders. She joked that to get the cancer in her mouth she must have laughed a lot in the sunshine.

I phoned her in Germany. She was miserable and wasn't sure of the treatment, the enemas, the juices. I think they had researched alternative therapies but there is so much more information now than there was in 2003. I think she was lonely and missing people, so she came home. I really didn't know much about cancer treatment then, but all I remember was pain, side effects, and the constant disappointment and disillusion of her care. The worst was when her oncologist told her there was nothing more they could do and to go out and enjoy the time she had left. Boy was she angry. Being young she had received lots of medical attention when first diagnosed and then when all their knowledge and further treatments dried up, she said they dropped her like a stone. Those were her words at the time and she felt so let down but not quite alone, she had so many friends that loved her dearly. Jo was a party person and knew everyone it seemed and all of them seemed so cool: DJ's, clubbers, musicians, with three young children I was on the periphery. I went to a huge fundraiser for her treatment in Germany. She looked amazing and beautiful and always so pleased to see me. It was a great night, a lot of love in that venue but as we hugged on arrival she winced in pain from the tumour on her back.

I was in awe of her smile and bravery. I remember bumping into her in X-ray when my daughter was eight months old.. I had overdone it and was very sick. I later collapsed in the doctor's surgery with pneumonia taking back my X ray results. I was ambulanced back to hospital and stayed a week there. I forgive that GP for making me go to hospital that day carrying Annabelle in her car seat, she obviously did not realise I was so ill. Anyway, after all that Jo had endured she greeted me so warmly in that X-ray waiting room, like an angel sent to help me. She was loud, making light of us both being sick, laughing and shining beauty and radiance probably much to the annoyance of the other miserable people waiting.

I tried to visit her when I could. On one of those occasions I walked into her bedroom and the atmosphere was tense with pain. Jo was having a soothing massage from a friend but she was not comfortable, trying to rest. I asked what I could do. She replied "anything please". I felt things were really bad so I did what I do when things are bad. I prayed out loud and held her hand. Jo was not religious and I wasn't sure how it would go down but did it anyway and the strange thing was when I came to the bit "Now at the hour of our death, Amen", well Jo sat bolt upright and said "That's enough I'm fine". It was Jo saying "F*ck that, I'm not going to die in the next hour". Or it was the miracle of prayer that lessened her pain. Not sure which, I will ask her when I see her again.

I really thought that death was imminent that night so went back the next day with the kids to say goodbye and as I pulled up outside her house full of foreboding, there she was at the window one hand in the air waving the other on the vacuum cleaner. What the hell?

That is cancer, each day is different.

Not long after that I could see it was becoming increasingly difficult for her husband (to be) as he was having to go to work and leave her all day, and her breathing was becoming a problem. So I sat with Jo and said that to ease his worry she should go to the hospice. Through my experience with my uncle at the hospice I had seen the extraordinary care he had been given, the relaxed atmosphere, the peace and tranquillity. She had to think about it but agreed in the end. She had a side room with a bird feeder outside her window. Sometimes I would go and the room would be filled with friends and other times it would just be the two of us. Jo was fascinated by Annabelle and used to come and visit her and enjoyed feeding her, so I took Annabelle to see her. She actually learnt to walk in Jo's room. Annabelle definitely bought something magical to that little room.

I think Jo and Kieran were planning to get married before her diagnosis and plans went ahead. She rang me for advice on a venue and I told her my favourite place in the world was The Orchard Tea room in Grantchester, a ramshackle place set in a mature orchard with old deckchairs and rickety tables arranged under the branches. In springtime before the tourists descended was my favourite time to visit. With the blossom weighing the branches down, just glorious. I had a particular spot where I would sit and think of my grandfather. He had told me he went there in his youth. I pictured him walking from Cambridge when he was studying history at Sidney Sussex. He probably had just enough for a scone and tea and made it last a whole afternoon whilst he debated some point with other students before the long walk back along the river bank…blissful, I would say.

She phoned as soon as she got there to say it was perfect and I think booked it there and then.

Kieran is Indian and Jo decided on saris for her and her bridesmaids. She was very happy that day, choosing which colour and showed me pictures of the fitting.

I visited one day and walked into a room full of friends crowded round her bed all looking anxious, the tension hit me like a smack in the face. I felt protective and alarmed. "Right, what's going on? Let's get some music on and open the window for Christ's sake", the whole atmosphere changed and everyone took action to clear the negativity and fear that had enveloped everyone like a weird spell.

Another visit and it was just me and her and she was so tired. I had this idea to take her on an imagination journey to a favourite spot, The Anchor pub garden, which was just on the river bank in Cambridge, the bit where people turn the punts around or go on further down the river to Grantchester. I described everything on a walk there. I really got into it and after I had finished she smiled and said quietly "you've made a difference". At that moment we were completely connected and I felt I had known her forever.

Meanwhile I was training for a fundraiser bike ride to raise money for the Hospice. Jo was constantly on my mind. I had left her side reluctantly the day before and on seeing her best friend I said they needed to move the wedding forward and she agreed. Whilst riding on my bike I got a call fromLlittle Jo, her bestie, to get to the hospice straight away. The wedding was going ahead that day at the hospice. I was asked to bring flowers and the bridesmaid's saris. So I did as well as dressing me and the kids. I stopped at a roadside flower van and bought a bouquet of sunflowers, her favourite.

I arrived to a flurry of almost silent activity. The wedding was to take place in the open air courtyard in the middle of the hospice. It had been transformed into a perfect wedding venue, a miracle created by the amazing staff. Sunflowers everywhere, hundreds of them. Tea lights creating a beautiful atmosphere. We had to wait a long time until Jo felt strong enough. Her bed was wheeled in and the ceremony went ahead. It took for ever for Jo to reply "I do". I think Kieran made a joke of the time it took her to reply.

I can't remember what happened after the ceremony. I think I was distracted by the children and the whole thing was so surreal. Only the people that attended would understand how beautiful that day was. We left and were called back the next day. I took my mum. We held back outside the room but were ushered in by her friends. I remember Kieran saying to Jo "come on, you got what you wanted, we are married, and you can go now, it's ok". The room was packed but we were pushed forward. My mum placed an angel in Jo's hand and told her what it was. Jo was laying on her side, seemingly asleep, but she tightened her hand around that little angel. I told her I loved her and we left. We had just got home and then Little Jo called to say she had gone. I went back in and sat with her. She really did look peaceful. I chatted to her for a little while. What was supposed to be her wedding venue turned into her wake venue. A huge giant poster of Jo stood amongst the trees, everyone wore their wedding outfits, the speeches were beautiful and I can't remember feeling sad.

I was in TK Maxx with Archie, to get pyjamas for Marley's surgery and bumped into Kieran (Jobug's husband), which felt so meaningful as I hadn't seen him for years. I burst into tears and he hugged me for ages but I just couldn't talk. Eventually with shoppers looking at me, I told him about Marley and his choice to refuse chemo. He was shocked and gutted that we were having to deal with cancer and from the conversation we had I still got a lot of anger 15 years on about conventional cancer treatment and the side effects Jo had suffered because of it. I felt Jobug had arranged that meeting to reassure me.

Darling Jobug

Aunty Joy

Written in February 2018

On Monday it is Aunty Joy's funeral and I still hurt every time she comes in to my thoughts. Joy battled with cancer for eight years. It started off as breast cancer. She was then diagnosed with ovarian cancer, which did not make sense to me, as she had a hysterectomy previously. She had so many disappointments, setbacks and in her last year everything spiralled down and I think she had had enough. The cancer was now in her liver and kidneys. The last lot of experimental chemo had taken her hearing and made her so sick. She was told a few times by the consultant that she was still alive due to her positive "get on with it" attitude. I only ever heard her complain once or twice about her consultant or her symptoms and to cheer her up I immediately went out and got her name tattooed on my wrist. This small act did make her happy.

The day before she died Annabelle and I whizzed down to see her. I woke up in the morning and felt a need to go. I wanted to support her daughter who had cared for her for so long and just spend time with her. Joy's daughter, Sharon, had tried to get her into a hospice the week before, but they were full so she was in Watford General and she was moved from ward to ward in those last weeks as no one knew what to do with her.

She looked very small, curled up in the hospital bed. I leant in close and said in her ear that I was there. She opened her eyes and turned over and was pleased to see us. She didn't stop moving and could not get comfortable and kept being sick, not food though, her poor stomach did not know what was happening any more and she was vomiting faeces. We took turns to pass her water and sick bowls, water to rinse her mouth. We closed the curtains to give her some privacy. She still managed to smile and ask about Marley and his Dad. I told her I was writing a book about Marley and I said she was going to be in it. She said "Am I?" in her quiet, humble way. We stayed about an hour trying to help her get comfortable.

We both cried all the way home. I asked God if he was going to take her, to take her quickly…and now she is gone. She died the next night on a full ward, with no privacy apart from a thin paper curtain. Joy was one in a million, so kind, understanding, loving and full of fun, and should have had a better place to die. There was not a private side room available for her and her husband and children to be together when she took her last breath. It's taking some time for me to release the anger about this, but I take comfort in the fact that by then Joy was so accepting of everything that she would have accepted it in her humble way and probably so relieved to be free of her poor body, so messed up from chemicals.

A month or so before she died she had been interested in Marley's diet and protocols. She couldn't keep anything down though by then, but she bought some organic soup that is probably still in her pantry. I never wanted to interfere with her treatment as that is what she had chosen at the time, many years before, but would she have chosen that option in retrospect? The rollercoaster of being told she was cancer free then it returning somewhere else. The consultants who didn't read her notes before meetings, the mix-ups between the different departments. Who knows? She did live long enough to see her granddaughters in their early years and they brought her a lot of pleasure. In my opinion, I think she died too soon and that she would have still been alive today if she had had the knowledge and understanding that we have gained since Marley's journey began. I think it is just like Chris Wark and many other cancer patients say, that once you sign up you can lose control over your life and body and it can be a series of unfortunate events on a cancer conveyor belt of treatment and medication and new unexpected treatments and horrors because of side effects from chemo or surgery.

I totally respect people's decisions and above all if you are going to choose conventional cancer treatment you have to believe in it. I do know people that did just that and who are not only survivors but thriving too.

With Aunty Joy May 2017

Chapter Four: Personal letters and perspectives from the family

A letter of thanks to Marley's Oncologist

Dear Han

Please accept this gift from Marley. You have to as it was the last thing he bought on this earth the day of his passing. He waited a year to receive money for his diagnosis from the government and it came into his account that day and so he spent his afternoon, with huge effort leaning his head back to gain a breath before typing in his order. He had fun ordering for his brother, sister and finally for you.

Marley had the greatest respect for you and your support and care made a difference in his life.

I miss my wonderful son but feel he is with me, guiding me.

I truly believe Han that Marley could have healed himself if the tumour had been anywhere else. At the time of his death the cancer had not metastasised. His blood, liver, kidneys were all clear and considering the tumour had ruptured on removal during surgery last November, I think that is a pretty impressive illustration of his detoxing protocols.

This cancer journey I did with Marley has taught me so much. A world away from my life as a child-minder before. We both spent hundreds of hours researching this year.

My most important lesson I have learnt just like the fundamentals of childcare is that as each child is unique and should be treated accordingly, so is each person's cancer but impossible to treat individually in the current system.

As a mother I look back and know from my research that there are things I did, didn't do that could have impacted on my son's health. I do not feel bad because I did the best I could with the knowledge I had at the time and I know that I have a better understanding on the consequences of what we put into our bodies, a better understanding of the importance of exercise and finding strategies and tools to help with our emotions to keep stress from impacting on our health.

Han I know first hand, from working for Debbie, how hard you all work for the best care for your patients. Completely dedicated to helping your patients survive but burdened with an ever increasing workload of new patients that you probably do not get the time to research new evidence. So I have included the second present Marley purchased for you, Chrisbeatcancer. He has spent 14 years researching for better outcomes and it is an easy read with many research papers listed in the back for evidence.

Educating patients and your cancer nurses on better nutrition will produce better outcomes and lessen the effects from treatment. Get rid of the sugar in the treatment centre café/shop and replace with foods that are healthy. Cold pressed juices, Green tea, nuts and fruit.

I have learnt that there is a cancer revolution going on all around the world, people taking responsibility for their disease and healing themselves and when the tests come back one thing resonates for all of them, that the oncologist (mainly in USA) is just not interested in the protocols and openly aloof which is confusing and understandable at the same time.

My son died, yes, but did not have one illness, not even a cold, not one stay in hospital. Not one prescription in all that time. From all of what I have learnt, of the testimonials from survivors and people living with cancer, surviving and thriving there is no way I cannot follow up Marley's request to you the day before he died, to educate your nurses and patients and remove the sugar from the café. All of this is from my heart and with the greatest respect.

Kind regards

Anne Marie Hoare

A letter of thanks to Marley's Surgeon

|Dear Miss Begum

I am writing on behalf of my family and friends to express our gratitude for the care and treatment of our son Marley.

Marley came to you in Sep 2017 with A Malignant Nerve Sheath Tumour on his vagus nerve.

You and your team operated on him on the 9th November. He recovered quickly and had already made a decision for no further conventional cancer treatment.

Marley had extensively researched evidence based protocols and was 100% dedicated to heal the cancer naturally and did incredibly well changing his lifestyle, nutrition, supplements also including a strict exercise programme of Cross Fit yoga and meditation.

Our amazing son passed away on September 24th. The rare and aggressive Triton cancer that was found within the original PNST was too much and the CT scan he had at the end of August confirmed it's regrowth.

He referred to this brief period before his operation as his first "dying time".

Miss Begum, the day of the operation many hundreds of people around the globe were praying for you, your team and Marley. We all knew the importance of the vagus nerve and how skilled you would have to be to not damage that nerve in any way. We all gave thanks at the end of that gruelling 6 hours that Marley incredibly gave us the "Thumbs up".

Yes our Son died he was given a prognosis of 50/50 with treatment and a year to live without. But we took those odds and he lived and died how he wanted.

At the time of his death the cancer had not spread to any other organ, his bloods were good and as you recall the 13cm tumour ruptured during the extraction. He had not one visit to the doctor or hospital stay. He was physically strong and was still doing pull ups weeks before his death. The tumour grew upwards and crushed his windpipe.

You gave us 10 quality months with Marley and although the toughest year, Marley never regretted his choices and said in the hospice that he had had a wonderful year.

Please pass on our thanks to the team and please remember always you made a difference in his life and consequently all of ours by your expert skill, care and human kindness. November the 9th will always be known as "Begum Day".

Kind regards

Anne-Marie and Andrew Hoare

A Sister's perspective

By Annabelle Hoare

Marley was eight when I was born, so growing up I don't remember having as much of a close relationship with Marley as my brothers did with each other. However like most siblings we still hung out, and I would go see him at university and we had a good bond.

When Marley came home from university, something in him changed. We would talk all the time and he would give me advice and choose to be with me to keep me company. The love and time he gave always made me happy and I appreciated it so much. He started coming to family parties and events with us out of his own choice; and stayed for more than 20 minutes! Whereas previously it would be a "Hi. Bye" situation. Everyone loved it. My uncle Villi said to me that Marley was a confident, hilarious, young boy, but as he went into his teens he slowly became more withdrawn. However in his last year he saw the happy, spontaneous Marley again. This is how we all now remember him.

In about 2015 I finally got Christened and chose Marley, Aunty Joy and my mum's friend, Luciana, to be my godparents, Mum really felt I should choose Marley to be my godfather and it now gives me another reason to love him even more.

I found it very hard in year 10 at school (14/ 15 years old) due to difficult relationships with my peers and teachers and anxiety. I didn't show it very often but I would dread to go into lessons and school in general, but Marley taught me how important education is and how he realised this when researching about his protocol. I strived to do my best in subjects and to stay focussed, and to change how people in school saw me. I wanted to leave Sawston Village College where teachers remembered me as the girl who turned a new leaf. I joined the school council and did assemblies for younger years. Marley made it so important that I knew the value of education and cheered me on. I enjoy school now!

My form tutor has been very supportive through Marley's diagnosis and since Marley's death. Her mum had passed away from cancer in 2014. It was nice to talk to someone who wasn't in my family about close relations dying.

I grieved before Marley died because I was able to express to her my fears and sadness about what would happen if he were to die. And I think this made it easier when he did die. I obviously didn't know it would help at the time, but it took away a lot of the stress because I accepted the fact he could die.

On the Sunday morning, 23rd September, I remember all of the family coming to visit Marley in the hospice. Marley was absolutely knackered, yet he got up and went out into the meeting area. My little cousin Emmanuel ran and jumped up on Marl to give him a hug. Marley simply said hello to everyone else, gave my Grandma a kiss, and then went back to his room quietly to rest as he was too tired. I remember it being a rainy day, not nice at all. But it meant me and Marl talked all day and planned what we wanted to do for the future and he promised he would still be here by my birthday on October 17th. We said that the next morning we would go to town and buy some nice things, so that morning I got him an oxygen tank, and a wheelchair. Marley decided he did not feel well enough to leave the hospice, but we did some online shopping instead, although as I bought the tank in to the room he said, "Annie I want to stand outside". So I took the oxygen tank and stood by the door, but far away enough so he could have some privacy. Aunty Sarah and I waited, watching him as he looked up at the sky. I can remember it so clearly. As he turned around it was though a bright golden halo was around him, like something from the movie Twilight. Marley wasn't a strong preacher to God but when he faced Sarah and me she said, " Marley, Gods' all around you". He replied "I know". I'll never forget this morning, or this day. It was like Marley had chat with God and knew he was going to die. My faith for god grew because I knew he was there in the room, and in our house, and with Marley throughout this whole time, since birth, helping and guiding him.

I did have my queries about God. Long chats with my Aunty Sarah and cousin Gracie at night helped me to answer questions I had. I was confused about why God would take away my brother just as we got so close. Where my Aunty Sarah simply replied along the lines of, " If he wasn't diagnosed would you have been so close? God made you so close that the memories you have of him are happy" and this was so true! I still ask questions to my mum like "what if this?'' or "what about?". But there's no further questions, what happened to Marley happened. He did have a short life, but for the time he was on this earth I believe he became a better person through his disease and left everyone happy in his last year. Whether it was the family, his best friend Dom, or the nurses at the hospice, he changed people and changed my perspective on the world. He was still so kind to people when he could've been mean and he remained positive when I couldn't see any light. For that reason I try to stay the happiest I can be, knowing my brother is around me no matter what. Why should I be sad when my brother was facing death right in the eyes, and was still worried about me, not putting himself first. The most poignant thing he said to me in the hospice was when I said I wasn't hungry and he assumed it was because I was sad, which I was, but I didn't want to show that. He looked at me with tears in his eyes and said, "Please don't be sad Annie! As long as I'm happy you can be too.'' I wanted to be okay for my mum, my dad, and my brothers and for myself. I went back to school very quickly and rose to all challenges when I maybe should've taken a bit more time to understand what had just happened. But I was confused, and wanted to erase it from my memory, when I know now it's a part of me and will stick with me forever and I see Marley as a hero.

Saying that, you need to go with the flow, do whatever feels best for you! However, if you let death control your life, it will. If you let it benefit you to become a better stronger person it can. I am so lucky that Marley died in the way in which he did. It happened quickly so he wasn't in too much pain. I was able to say goodbye and to say I love you over and over again. Everything we needed was provided and we always seemed to be in the right place at the right time.

Not everyone has that.

That's why I look for the best in every possible situation. Start saying yes, start thinking; am I an inspiration to those around me? Can I be? Can I use this horrible thing that's happened to me to help others? I think you can.

Yes I am young, but I have gained a vast amount of maturity through grief and the best advice I can give is to seize all opportunities you have with your loved ones. Try to forgive people's pasts, and take care of yourself just as much.

About a week after Marley passed I went into school and wanted to tell my closest friends, about 10 of us, as they were the ones who helped me. We all sat on the school field and I said how he passed away. Many cried and some just looked at me silently. What would you say?

We sat for a while longer and I thanked them for helping me and said how much Marley appreciated their support. We had a group hug. Then I left.

They have never stopped supporting me.

Wednesday 12th June 2019.

It's almost 9 months since Marley died. I am still trying to be as happy as I can. But I realised, not coming to terms with your emotions and just carrying on faking supreme happiness is not always inspirational. Inspirational is going through all of the emotions: happiness, sadness, loneliness, anger, love, fear, vulnerability, everything, yet you still wake up every day thinking 'lets do this!'

I do think there is slight PTSD from Marley's death. The feeling everyday that I have to text my close friends and family 'I love you', just so that the last thing I may have said to them was positive. Having a constant vivid flash back of not being able to stop my brother from dying. Guilt is a feeling you gain sometimes after a death. It is something I need to work on. A mind-set that is easy to gain but, just as easy to loose.

I am 16 years old with lots to learn, many more ships to guide and a long life ahead of me, but I know my worth and my aim in life. And I'm ready to live for those who have died.

Thursday 4th July 2019.

All of my GCSE exams are now done, and I have been celebrating because I did better than I thought. I prayed every night to God and Marley, as I was so anxious, and I really felt he was there helping me.

Last Friday I had my prom and had a lovely time! Like most people who grieve, I get sad when thinking about Marley and Aunty Joy not being at life's milestones, so I felt very sad that Marley wasn't there. However I knew he was watching.

My friend Federico and I at the school prom.

My three best friends; Adam, Ellie and Alfie

Recently I have been really struggling, but I've felt Marley's presence so strongly. When I get sad I feel like Marley's saying 'you'll feel better in the morning' and giving me a hug.

Sometimes you wish you could bring people down from heaven to spend the day with them. Hug them, laugh with them, cry with them, listen to them, and hear their voice, pay millions of pounds just to be able say to them "I love you" over and over again and hear them say it back in person not just in your head.

My friends have been very supportive in many different ways. They drag me outside to distract me from sadness or just surround me with love when they know I don't want to talk. I never seem to actually cry. It's always on the inside. I have realised to acknowledge my feelings and be okay with the fact I am allowed to cry as I have lost my brother, but I still cant. It's so true about 'riding the wave', referring to life's challenges, you never know what the next day holds.

Friday 3rd January 2020.

Today I watched Little Women, an unusual choice of film for me.

I'm sure many of you have read the book and felt a lot of love towards the four very different girls, Meg, Jo, Beth and Amy.

The main character, Jo, goes through a lot of heartache, fear, and rejection. However what struck me most was her reaction to the loss of her sister Beth, as it reminded me of myself when Marley died confused, angry, but still full of love and hope, even though she, Jo, was so frustrated that it seemed bad things kept happening to her.

Beth caught scarlet fever and had time to acknowledge that she was going to die.

She said to Jo when they were at the seaside;

"It's like the tide. Even though it may go out slowly, you can never stop it from happening. "

I'm sure Marley saw this analogy similarly, as I did too.

Recently I have been trying to be honest with my true feelings towards life.

I am happy and grateful and positive about what has happened in my life. It could be worse. But it isn't worse. I have a family who, like any other family, has differences and selfish arguments. Parents who are together but sometimes question whether they want to parent together. The insecurities of a 17-year-old girl, and the loss of a friend, an aunty, and a brother.

I wake some days to a burst of happiness and feel as though I will never look back on sadness. Yet the next day I wake up without being able to sit up, as the world feels like it's on my chest. I am doing my best living for my brother, focusing on what we shared through love of music. I want to sing. Make happiness out of sadness, for I have been through sadness, so I will sing about joy. Or at least with joy in my heart, in my eyes, in my memories and in my brother.

It's okay to wake up in the middle of the night because you're scared over the thoughts you're having. It's also okay to not cry in situations where society may judge you because you should be crying. I still am finding it hard to ask for help from people, and seek love where I know it can be found. As I am like Jo, I don't want to be hurt again. I'm fed up of being let down, and I don't want to be turned away.

I still speak to Ellie often as we go to the same new college, where I'm studying Media, Music, and Photography. For the first time I really do love school, but I miss my friends. I miss Adam and Alfie, who are both at a different college from me. Summer 2019 at the time felt like the worse summer ever, but I was blind to the fact I was surrounded by so much love, and happiness from the people I care about most. We were all aware of each other's different anxieties and depression, but instead of addressing it, we allowed the feelings to come and go whilst being a hand for each other.

Summer 2019 itself changed so much for me and I will never forget the fun I had.

Even though Ellie and I may not see Adam and Alfie for months at a time, when we meet up again it feels like we were never apart. I'm sure will be the same when I see Marley or Joy again. Thoughts like this keep me going. The new friends I make at college and work keep me going. Everyday I learn a little more about myself, keep my motivation, and just allow myself and others to take time in the things they're doing.

Archie is living in Brighton, as I'm sure he feels close to Marley there. I miss him and its weird not having either of my brothers at home, but we are still close and keeping on going.

Good luck everybody. Spread love.

BIG LOVE

Marley's brother Archie

Archie has tried to do a piece for this book but is stuck. It's too hard for him, but no doubt one day he will put together an exhibition of art or something that he finds an easier way to express his feelings about the loss of his brother. But for now, I will put in this recent photo of him, taken by his sister. He is well and happy, has moved twice and now living in a nice apartment near his new job, caring for a gentleman with additional needs. He wanted to move to Brighton to feel closer to Marley but kept holding back, worried about leaving us. So I had to have a hard talk with him, to release him of that. We see him when we can and talk all the time. He eats well and knows the score on healthy eating and a healthy lifestyle? Well that I can't answer but I know his brother will be watching over him.

Archie in Brighton next to someone's graffiti about his brother

Marley's Dad, Andy, was the same as Archie. He wants to support this book but finds it too hard. We are all different and find different ways to cope, but Andy agreed to put his Eulogy in, which I think is pretty perfect and he knows that through Marley's diagnosis, healing and then his death, he could not cope, he was in denial and struggles most days with the loss, but when Marley told him his intentions to refuse chemo and radiotherapy his initial response was complete agreement, which was such a blessing for Marley.

The Eulogy written and read out by his Father

Time sometimes feels like it is moving fast, sometimes slow.

I'm not sure which I prefer or whether we have a choice. Some things like a beautiful summer day. 2018, I believe has been the best summer of my life and perhaps the worst, a bit torn. That fresh spring morning with new life everywhere in nature.

Last winter I walked miles and miles through the snow, thinking deeply about Marley's condition, (my amazing son) and how he was fighting it so bravely. I will always be so proud of him and his courage in his choosing of a natural healing approach. I crunched through the snow, choosing the deeper more enduring path, some paths we walk are supposed to be hard, if not sometimes some lessons are not learnt. I feel like I have just learnt the hardest lesson. But I feel peaceful, an almost blessed feeling of having had time, 25 wonderful years with our son.

On the 24th September some photos turned up in the afternoon at the hospice, found in an old cook book. They were a series of photos of Marley at 6 weeks old. Looking at them made me feel uncomfortable as I knew what they were but hadn't seen them in 25 years. We were visiting my Dad who lived in Swanage. On the drive down we had stopped to see my Nan. She loved seeing Marley for the first time but said he had looked poorly. We were unknowing. That evening his little lungs collapsed due to bronchiolitis and we went to Poole hospital. That night was long, he lay in a little cot with breathing apparatus, his Mum (beautiful Mum) watching over him. These photos were the same scene as the 24th September 2018. I do remember feeling very sad. "If he makes it through the night, he may survive". (A fine delivery of words from a professional.)

I was very worried, I remember the feelings, my words, expression. I prayed Marley was always strong and life got great, 25 years of great.

These photos troubled me that day, I find some omens uncomfortable.

Marley passed away that evening. We were none of us expecting it. This was six weeks after his 25th birthday. The thing I learnt was that he could have been taken from us at only six weeks, if so, half my life would have never been so blessed and that 25 years was a huge bonus, and I feel privileged to have loved and lost him now, than to not have experienced his beautiful being.

May your God's bless you all and keep your families and loved ones equally safe and protected.

The Eulogy written and read at Marley's funeral by Tracey, Marley's support worker from CLIC sargent .

I met Marley a short while after the surgery that confirmed his cancer diagnosis. The consultant responsible for the TYA service at Addenbrookes had expressed to me her concern for this young man who had refused further treatment; she wanted me (in her words) to "work my magic" to see why and to see whether we could convince him otherwise. However, within seconds of talking on the phone with Marley, I heard this overwhelming passion, and sensed his belief in his decisions. We spent a long time talking about the many studies he had read and research he had done, and I was completely blown away. He was alive, enthused, informed, impassioned.

When we spoke of his next hospital appointment, that passion and belief disappeared, and he became quiet and said that he didn't really see much point; he felt the medical team thought he was "silly" and that he did not know what he was doing or talking about. I explained that this was not the case, it was just very unusual for a young man to go against the traditional medical model of cancer treatment, and this had thrown everyone into an unfamiliar situation.

We discussed how to deal with this, and agreed that he needed to use his next appointment as an opportunity to demonstrate the depth of his knowledge, and that he *was* making informed and educated decisions. And this is exactly what he did! In that meeting, with conviction and passion, Marley explained his most important findings, articulated how they had lead him to the choices he had made, and convinced the medical team to walk alongside him, to support him rather than oppose his wishes. He was able to meet their minds, and demonstrate how, while they could not necessarily agree on Marley's model of treatment, they could agree to disagree in a respectful, kind and compassionate way.

This I believe is Marley's legacy!

Over the months that followed, I got to know what an inspiringly open, kind, warm, funny, compassionate, thoughtful and reflective young man he was. Even when he was met with differing opinions on his choices, he always, always put himself in their position to understand and explain their behaviour. His patience and compassion in his beliefs were inspiring.

I will very much miss our discussions and debates of the pros and cons of religion, spirituality, veganism and even the Rajneeshees!!

Marley is, and I'm sure will *always* be, the most courageous young man I have ever met. He made choices to do things his way knowing the risks and I'm not so sure there are many people in this world that have the courage to do that.

I was constantly asking him to consider having a "wish" (a charity funded event tailored to his own interests) but all he would ever say is that he doesn't need anything as he has been blessed with the most amazing family and friends, and his life is rich enough.

The last time I saw Marley, he told me that he was at peace with the choices he had made, that he was ok about everything and that he had had a wonderful life.

The day after Marley passed there was the most wonderful sunset and I stood and watched for a long time thinking about Marley, and then somehow this epitaph came to mind:

An honest man here lies at rest, The friend of man, the friend of truth, The friend of age, and guide of youth:

Few hearts like his, with virtue warmed, Few heads with knowledge so informed;

If there's another world, he lives in bliss; If there is none, he made the best of this.

(Robbie Burns)

Chapter Five: Epilogue

29th November 2018

So here I am 8 weeks after my son's death, his giant pictures still hanging up. I think I have thanked all the people I needed to for their love, care, food and a thousand kind gestures. I still have to compose a thank you to all the people that donated to the Just Giving page my sister set up. Finding that one hard.

Andy and I take turns in crumbling in grief, mostly first thing as we wake and remember or in the evening. A week or so back, despite putting in place all the things I know to help; a rough plan of the day, exercise, juicing and good food, the company of friends, I came back home and spiralled down a well of pain. Archie joined me and we could not control it. Eventually I dragged us both out, swollen eyes and all to get some fresh air and something to eat. Archie was frustrated because he said that crying was not healing and he must be doing something wrong. Later on I asked him how he now felt? I definitely felt calm and more relaxed. He agreed but I made a decision that day that I didn't deserve that sort of emotional pain so for now I have put Marley in a place in my heart and when I choose I go somewhere quiet and open the door. For now my happiness is in work and keeping busy. I start work properly after Christmas but see all my families regularly thank goodness.

Writing this book helps, volunteering helps, our puppy helps.

I have cleaned every cupboard, every drawer and cleared the clutter. It was unintentional really, I just lost my sh*t one day, as I could not find my glasses and anger turned to healing through cleaning.

I have read two books on the afterlife. I have been to see a past-life therapist. That was very interesting but I haven't figured anything out yet and I am still completely confused. All my opinions and thoughts on what happens next have changed. So I have no advice on grief, It's just like the cancer experience, everyone is unique and there are two choices really.

1. Go to a dark place and stagnate in a pool of bitterness, anger and sadness for the rest of your life.

2. Live your life as best you can, helping as many people as you can.

I am really going to try for option 2. I have work to do. After seeing for myself how nutrition can have such a positive effect on cancer patients, I have to, at the very least, get the sugar out of the cancer treatment waiting room. Get the hospital nutritionists up to date with the latest research to help get better outcomes for all cancer patients. I also want to volunteer at the hospice and do anything for CLIC Sargent. I'm on a mission!

One of my charges, myself and Louis with money raised from Souper Fridays in our village. The whole community and Big Love helped to provide weekly lunches throughout winter. Soup, bread, tea and cakes. People attended from near and far and it was a great distraction for me.

10th July 2019

It's been just over nine months and some days, mostly weekends, especially Sunday, the pain is so overwhelming and just as intense as when Marley died. Just like my daughter I am going with the flow and if I feel bad I go with it and know it is temporary and let emotions flow. The anger, the sadness, the total loss. Other days I get up and appreciate the still of the morning, my dog and rabbit, free in the garden before anyone else wakes up. I sit in my camp chair with the sun on my face, drinking tea with Louis on my lap who is watching Binky the rabbit intently. I listen to the birds and I feel close to Marley and to God. I take this time to be quiet and listen to what is going on in my mind and turn worries or negative thoughts around. I run early in the morning up and over Coploe hill and back, sometimes I reach the peak and I am overwhelmed by the beauty of the view unfolding and that's where I take stock. I slow down, sometimes to a walk to take it all in, to stare at the beauty. Marley comes to mind, walking alongside or running as a seven year old along the hedgerows and laughing. There is a solitary tree in the middle of a field and to me and Annabelle it is Marley tree. For some reason I visualise him coming out from behind it, smiling and waving.

I have attended spiritual cafes with friends and strangers, and now I don't spontaneously sob in the guided meditations. I find them really relaxing and if Marley comes into my mind I feel a smile spreading on my face. His spirit gives me calmness, peace and a feeling like he is the patient teacher and I am the child still learning. I always visualise him in a beautiful garden, jungle like and he points out plants and flowers. I am glad I have been pushed to a path of spiritual discovery, of learning new things, new possibilities, of writing this book, however challenging.

My relationship with God is still up and down. Most days I am filled with gratitude for my life, for my family and friends, for lessons I am learning and for my job, as working with children is the greatest gift. Their joy is contagious. We go out in nature every day, which also is such a lift. I don't know how I would have survived in another profession. They talk about Marley in a matter of fact way which I appreciate. We were talking about one of their birthdays being the day before Marley's and how I wanted to celebrate. "But he is dead" one of them stated. With a smile I say, "I know he is dead but I still want to celebrate". I still write his name in birthday cards, why would I not include him? He is my family and always will be. A spiritual healer once told me that me and Marley connect mostly in the car, which is where we spent so much time together, driving to and from the hospital and Brighton. For a few months when I was alone driving the seat-belt alarm would go off and I felt it was him. It was lovely but then it stopped and I was a bit sad, then one evening Annabelle and Archie came to CrossFit with me and the alarm sounded the whole way there almost in happiness that we were doing something all together that made him happy. The noisy alarm could not drown out our laughing and happiness to feel his spirit. After that night me and Annabelle thought he had left us but during her exams that meant so much to her she felt his presence every day. Just last week I was cleaning his room, now Archie's, and as I dusted I just felt such a happy presence that grew stronger and made me smile. Again cleanliness and order made Marley happy and I felt it was making him happy for his room to be cleaned. When I told Archie what had happened he thought I was just giving him a hint to clean the room more. We have managed to keep Marley's herbs, peace lily and Aloe Vera plants alive. I have kept his last chillies he bought in the fridge. His Addidas sliders and Vans trainers are by the front door alongside our shoes and will always remain there.

I miss his gentle smile, his kind, comforting voice. His naughtiness and playfulness and strange random noises that all my kids seem to make. I miss his cooking so much, we all do. Not one of us has an appetite, it is just fuel and I can cope with making a meal maybe twice a week but have no inspiration. I mostly do juicing when I can then I know at least we have some nutrients down us. Archie came shopping with me for the first time in years and I was so glad as I find it very hard.

24rd September 2019, One year on

So the day is upon us. A strange countdown. I booked a villa in Ibiza, near to where Marley stayed just before he died. I put it on the credit card. The kids so needed a holiday. Somewhere beautiful, somewhere they could feel the sun on their faces. I was really pleased when Andy decided to come too.

Marley's best friend Dom came too. We wanted to thank him for the day trips he took Marley on. To obscure places of beauty, botanical gardens and art galleries, every Sunday during that last year. We also took Archie's friend Eliot, (also a chef, ha ha!) I couldn't wish for a better gang.

I didn't plan anything for today, I just went with the flow. It started with a new ritual of tea in bed then watching dawn in Ibiza. The mist rising, hearing cockerels in the distance. As the kids started to rise, the music that is so important to us all came on. We watched videos of Marley and I read his last text messages on WhatsApp. Marley's friend

Anna, who had helped him so much texted me and we arranged to meet up. We had a delicious banquet for breakfast, we toasted Marley. We found Anna in a secluded spot. We looked down from the cliff edge to see her standing on the rocks, waving. We clambered down, two strangers meeting, slightly embarrassed and awkward. A woman of my age with smiling eyes, a petite frame, T-shirt and shorts and cool sunglasses. I wanted to study her face and hug this woman, who meant so much to my son. Humble and dismissive to any thanks we gave her. "I did nothing", she said quietly. The cove was tiny and deserted, a shell and stone beach. Crystal waters that calmed us all and the kids went off to explore. We chatted and shared stories about Marley and filled in the gaps of his time there.

It was a perfect, calm and blissful retreat. We met up with Anna a few times and explored the Island on our own. We all connected and had fun and were toasted nicely by the sun. One morning we left the kids in search of a tree to plant as a memorial to Marley. We found a lovely road side place with a young Argentinian girl clearly moved by Marley's story who helped us find the perfect one. A palm exactly like the one outside his room and Anna let us put it in her garden.

6th January 2020

My editor Rachel, gently asked for another paragraph. A positive note, "looking forward maybe?" I can't promise that. I have a lot going on. Grieving is still very raw. I think you never get over loosing a loved one, you just slowly learn how to live without them as best you can.

We have travelled to Italy three times. I went with my friend. Frances paid for me and Rome awoke every sense, my appetite, my love of art. We travelled down to Naples and Capri. I didn't have to think for anyone else and I felt young, free and even got my water colours out and painted the coast whilst toasting my skin. I took Andy back to Rome 6 weeks later, and then a friend leant us his apartment near Bellagio in November. We had fun and were carefree driving the hair-pin bends in a little Audi. All the travelling was a wonderful distraction.

We have met with Marley's friends down in Brighton and stay firmly connected. We were surprised and touched by a record released by his friend Issac to raise money for CLIC Sargent.

We are still very fragile. Andy comes shopping with me every week as I still get massive anxiety walking into a grocery shop. Waitrose is a definite No No. Marley and I walked the isles together two to three times a week, but we manage Aldi. It's a new store and we pretend we are on holiday in Europe.

I love my job as always and I am surrounded by babies. It is crazy busy and I have no time to think.

Quite a few of us in the village are training to run the Cambridge Half Marathon in March 2020, in aid of the Arthur Rank hospice. I welcome the long runs on a Saturday with my friends. I go to circuits, meditate and do yoga occasionally. I still say affirmations, pray, work on this book to make it note-worthy and not boring so that Marley can give me a nod of approval.

I am ashamed to say I don't juice everyday, I have eaten loads of sugar over Christmas and bizarrely, even took up smoking the odd roll-up again and I still dislike cooking. I have possible anger issues and am probably not the greatest to live with BUT exercise definitely helps, I am wearing a nicotine patch, Andy is doing the cooking, I'm juicing more with the kids I look after and I am booked in for blood tests to test my hormones and booked in for anger management. I am taking responsibility!

It's still early days…..One day at a time……

I hope you put this book down and feel lifted though. Hopefully it opened your mind to new thinking about cancer healing and took away some of your fear of cancer and more than anything in this crazy life we live in, with the news papers and T.V spreading hate and fear, that you can be reassured that there is so much good in the world, so many people that want to help, that gather together to lift others and support each other.

Big Love always comes through

Souper Saturdays (In aid of the Arthur Rank hospice) February 2020, with my sisters and Biglove helpers

Chapter Six: Big Love

At the time of editing there were 17,000 posts on the Big Love Whatsapp group chat. Not just messages of love and encouragement, but pictures of beauty in nature, poems, quotes and videos to cheer me and our whole family up. We have picked up a couple of strangers on the way who needed some extra help. I am so honoured to be part of the Big Love movement.

The Transcript

21/08/2017, 5:46 pm - **Anne Marie: Karen suggested this as it's easier to let you all know.no news but my friend and client is an oncologist and pulled in favours she thinks he will have to go to Papworth because of the position for biopsy. They have a big meeting on Thursday and CT scan is booked for his head. I worked today and got through I don't know how, Archie took Marley to David Lloyd . Clare got them passes to relax in the Spa...I don't know how Marley feels I really don't. I feel so exhausted I can**

barely think. But a day at a time and not looking further than that.. Support from friends and family keeping us going. Keep thinking good thoughts xxx love you all

Dad: I am here I wish I could give you all my strength

Dad: Love you all x

Anne Marie: I have your strength

Karen: Well done darling .. this will be a great way to communicate easily, nothing worse than not knowing so amazing if some strings can be pulled and you get knowledge to tackle quicker ... you are surrounded with love .. anything .. anytime .. just ask xxx

Clare Sis: Bless you sweetheart if there is anything I can do like cook food give you a foot massage before bed?

Sharon: Anything you need, just ask xx

Jess: Thinking of you everyday. Please ask me if there's anything I can do to help I have a spare car and love to have Annie over anytime

Susie: Ditto. Love & prayers

Katie From Mill: Big love from all the Owens. We're here if you need anything at all. Xxx

Luciana: Thanks for the update my darling we are with you. Anything in the meantime say the word. Home tomorrow x

Helen: You have many many friends who love you all and willing to help. Use us! Don't try and do everything on your own. Sending love and prayers Hxx

Anne Marie: The greatest thing today was the Spa and hearing my boys laughing and being relaxed in a restaurant after...I don't want them in a bad mindset...so My sis Clare you are an Angel!!

Thank you all for sending love.

Susan H: Sending you lots of love Ann-Marie, thinking of you all xx

Catherine: Hey Anne Marie thank you so much for keeping us up to date. You know how much we love and value you and all your family. I have been slightly obsessively cooking you lasagne all evening, Justin will drop off on way through to Duxford, pls don't feel the need to chat, he'll just drop em outside. Mum reiterated offer of Norfolk if and when for some respite. Love you all a million billion xxx

Clare Sis: That's a LOVSAGNA

Shirley: Hey sweetie, I have deliberately decided NOT to cook you anything - cos I love you all too much....!

However, there is always a jug of Cosmo waiting for you here - any time.....

Anne Marie: When good news comes I'll be in that jug x

Shirley: Oh, bugger it. I'll make it in an ice bucket so we can both fit in.... xxxx

Helen M: Make it a Jacuzzi so we can all fit in!!

22/08/2017Anne Marie: Hello my loves Biopsy tomorrow morning at 9.30...we have to wait 10 days ish for results. CT head scan on Friday. xx he has had another lovely day relaxing and eating.

Thankyou for all the love and food....I love you all very much.

Shirley: So good that he's relaxing and eating!!!! And even better that the medics are cracking on with all of it.

Luciana: Best of luck my lovey! I'll drop some biscuits/flapjacks tomorrow xxx

Sharon Cousin: Thinking of you xxxxx

Rosie: Sending all my love for today Anne Marie.

Clare Sis: Thinking of you there in spirit and heart x

Susan: Have just lit a candle and said a prayer for you all at the most beautiful monastery at the top of a hill here in Menorca. You are all in our thoughts, sending you all our love xx

Anne marie: hello...long day but it went well and he has been resting...2 weeks till any news..x love you all

24/08/2017 Anne marie: Hello lovelies. The Biopsy yesterday was non diagnostic so Marley will have an MRI at Papworth next Thursday. All other scans cancelled. X Thanks for all your love.

Clare Sis: What does that mean????

Anne marie: You are not the only one. I did'nt take the call...The tissue sample was not good enough to diagnose...waiting for Debbie to translate properly.x

Anne marie: MRI is best all over scan.

Karen: Yeah it means not enough cells were taken to diagnose ... maybe a repeat ?

Clare Sis: So limbo?

Anne marie: no not limbo...I mean in limbo

Not do the limbo

Anne marie: I would rather do the Limbo

Shirley: I'll do the limbo with you!!!!   As long as someone can help me down and then help me back up again

30/08/2017, Anne Marie: basically a lot of specialists are all doing their best to sort a plan but the communication has been confusing...so the consultant is confirming the MRI tomorrow if not it will be at Addenbrookes on Sunday and a possible plan a week on Friday..Marley is doing OK and looks a lot better than when he arrived. We can only do "A day at a time".

Thanks for all the love ..it helps xx

Anne marie: MRI now on Sunday x

Helen Mo: how frustrating to have to wait longer!!! Let's hope it definitely happens then for you all xx

Anne marie: It will I'm sure they are doing their best...not frustrated. got to go with the flow.

Hells bells: Hope things went okay today, thinking of you xxx

Jess: Well done getting through today AM x

Anne marie: I think it's all the good thoughts coming our way x

plan to be discussed Friday afternoon.xxx

Aunty Joy: That's good .Start chemo again today Paul's here with the girls.

Lovely to see them all. Thinking of all Love you x

Clare Sis: Joy sending you a big warm cuddle from Clare xxx we all think of you everyday x

04/09/2017, 3:45 pm - Aunty Joy: Love you all

Karen: Let us know how you got on today xxx

Anne Marie: will do..in reception now...

Clare Sis: With you in heart and soul

Anne Marie: Well my dear friends I really wish I could say I have answers..

He had a camera up his nose then an unsuccessful biopsy that was awful to witness but he has recovered. It was a long afternoon. It is what it is...Saw the lump for the first time properly and it's huge but I really don't think it's cancer I just don't...the docs can't tell for sure but it's been there a long time growing.. They are doing their best I'm sure...phoning us at night..It's complicated in situation and size...It's going to be alright I just know it will..big hugs to all of you my wonderful pillars.

Anne Marie: So when we come tomorrow to the Icklestock festival no fuss no sympathetic looks...you know what I'm like! Annie is singing and Marley wants to see her.xx

Luciana: We are with you my lovely , I hope kisses, cuddles and smiles are allowed, and lots of support for Annie. Looking forward to seeing you all

Anne marie: Tomorrow is a day for celebration. we have a lot to be happy about

Susan: No fuss, just love and laughter as always. Can't wait to hear Annie sing, love you xx

Susie: Waiting without answers is so hard. You are doing great. Staying positive.

Jilly⬜: Dear, dear boy. Camera up the nose is no fun. He will be pleased to kick it into touch once they get a handle on it. Clare I hope your friends are ok. We will try to come tomorrow, good luck lovely Annabel.

Sharon Cousin: Thinking of you all. Please send my love to Marley, he's incredible. Send my love to Annabelle too, I wish I was there to hear her sing, she is amazing. You're all amazing! Love to you all xxxx

12/09/2017 Anne marie: Hello lovelies...so...Thursday PET scan and CT (radioactive glucose injected...cancer cells absorb it then show up on scan) in morning then more detailed MRI in afternoon to see how the lump is attached to nerve for surgery prep... results following week on Tuesday and Thursday. Marley has eaten well went to pictures last night with Archie and even made us all chilli last night...that makes

me happy. normal stuff!! Xx Thank you for all the messages

Luciana: Great to be getting some movement and hopefully some answers!! Lots of love and positive vibes

Jilly: Hang on in there, answers and a plan of action will not be far off, massive hugs to you all in the meantime, you are such a wonderful family xxx

Gracie Angel: Thanks for the info AM. More than I would get from Marley himself but that's classic him. Jealous of the chilli... bet it was great!!! He is such a good cook. Love to you all xx

Anne Marie: home again! Efficient service again..he's eaten 2 crossants and a huge pretzel and a kale juice ...makes me happy...I'm a feeder!!

14/09/2017 Anne marie: We are having an Indian banquet with thanks to DJ and vegan cookies which I presume are from Marley's only Vegan in the village friend dear Sharon x

19/09/2017Anne marie: Hello angels. from PETscan there is a lot of fast activity which proves there will be a Cancer battle

but not 100% sure so he will go to royal Brompton hospital in Chelsea for biopsy and surgery/chemo or radiotherapy...asap....not Papworth because The Brompton more experienced with NF1.

He showed no emotion whatsoever....He is amazing and so brave or is not dealing with it. love you all...keep thinking good thoughts because I am

Susie: My niece has had heart surgery at the Brompton twice - all the staff there were amazing. I also have a very good friend who lives in Chelsea so anything you need locally...vegan bakery recommendations, a break from the hospital, Whatever! Just let me know.

Sharon Cousin: Brompton is one of the best hospitals in the world, Marley will be in excellent hands. Sending you all my love, especially Marley, he's amazing

Clare Sis: I have read amazing things on Brompton this afternoon it's cutting edge and such expertise in their field. There are no finer hands my nephew should be in. I've researched everything you might need every entrance to every wing every floor and lift to get you there quickest even parking meters or tube station or bus every visitors hour even the matrons on the ward and what to take so when you need it you have research folder of helpful tips ! I am calm and confident xxx

Shirley Clark: Never mind calm and confident Clare - you're bloody amazing!!!!

Shirley Clark: Hey Anne- Marie. This group should have been called Big Fat Love.......!!!

Anne marie: it's the best group in the world!!

Anne marie: So to celebrate his graduation we had delicious dumplings down Burleigh St after a relaxing acupuncture session...cheers☐we both agreed probably better than Graduation ceremony anyway.

Clare Sis: Yippee!!!! Congratulations x

Well done Marley!! He has so much to be proud of and look fwd to xxx

Gracie Angel: I did a little cheer for Marley where I know his name would have been sounds like he would enjoy that more than graduation anyway!!!!

Rosie Smith: Anne Marie if you need a place to rest in London you know you are welcome to come to our flat; hospital is 30 mins drive from here xx

Anne marie: Another tough rollercoaster day but not only did Adam the acupuncturist heal his terrible backache and anxiety he gave Marley a wonderful book bought by Paddy that he is happily reading now sipping his calorie drink...so many kindnesses all around...

Brompton on Friday but as long as he keeps drinking eating and spirits strong we are going to be ok.xx love to you all

Lisa: Another!! Focus w positive vibes for Friday!! Yes - there are some very kind people out there! So pleased he is relaxed - stay strong xx

Susie: Acupuncture is bliss! Yay for Marley! Gonna be a long week

Karen: Think you might be up for some extra love and cuddles for your Birthday ... can be sporadic and play by ear . but you know we can get on down last minute for you

Anne marie: Ahhh lovely thought but hold everything for the day there is good news about my boy then there will be a celebration!!

27/09/2017 Anne Marie: So my friends in this crazy horrific nightmare rollercoaster there is also wonderful moments of closeness, kindnesses beyond belief, family strengthened and funny moments too where we have laughed. Annabelle has been picked for an audition tonight ..put forward by her singing coach and if she gets it a full scholarship...so happy for her and lovely to see her bouncing off the walls.

Marley is getting stronger each day and preparing for what lies ahead...Thank you to you all for keeping me afloat with your love.

27/09/2017, 12:54 pm - Jilly☐: You have kept us afloat for years with the love you have lavished on all my babies so you deserve nothing less! So pleased for Annabel, how exciting!! Glad Marley is gaining strength from your loving care xxx☐☐

Catherine: What Jilly said too. You reap what you sew my friend. Really miss you Anne Marie, next time I catch you you are getting a bone crusher from me and of course to Marley, so pleased you are building him up xxxx

Clare Sis: Once upon a time there was a little baby boy born whose name was Marley he was born to a crazy arsed family that loved him with all their heart

Anne marie: Don't freak out....we have to wait til next thursday...the bloods were not done in time...it is God's will We are actually "om"...Marley is accepting and so are we. There has to be a reason for this ..even if it's to build him up an extra week.

Clare Sis: Right

Shirley: They are taking the f*cking piss

Karen: There is always a reason .. but holy moly that is properly rubbish thank god Marley is so chilled .. xxx

I think the person in charge of bloods should have a bollocking !!

Anne marie: We still want that love cake Jilly!!

Jilly: It is winging its way to you xxx

Helen: What a bloody roller coaster for you guys, so sorry xx

Helen: Bugger!! X

Aisha: So sorry to hear this. Amazing to hear how strong & accepting you're all being, keep that positive attitude up

Catherine: Love cake sounds a bit dodgy, dudes. Only in Ickleton. Meat and vegan options on your door step this am so Archie should have em now .Your endurance is amazing so sorry there is more waiting involved amazing strength

Love as always mwah mwah

Gracie Angel: Birthday?! Happy birthday Anne Marie xxxx Marley rang me today - seemed to be in a great mood hope you all had a happy day xx

Anne marie: my bday is tomorrow and was totally going against my principal to know when to celebrate good things!! but my kids did'nt take any of my bullshit...so sweet and know me so well...awaiting dinner cooked by marley who miraculously came back(in spirit) to us today at the thought of moving out for a bit...could'nt be happier...Don't need or want a thing...nothing can top today !!

Happy Birthday girlie girl!!!!

It's a good day!!!!

Clare Sis: Happy birthday my amazing sister was one of the best nights of my life last night seeing Marley blossom and be funny sweet cheeky and want to cook

5/10/2017 Anne marie: Ok everyone it's happening for next 40 mins please pray...or say this for us "Marley is divinely guided and protected" That the consultant gets the cells he needs but leaves nerves and lungs protected...NZ family join hands and sing loud!!!

Rosie: Saying those words right now sending all our love

lisa :Over & over xx

Susie: We are with you in spirit May the lord bless you and keep you

Anne marie: He is out and looks good.

Clare Sis: And .... breathe

Anne marie: Can't express how much your messages kept me going today,

Results on Monday....xx

Catherine: Huge love to you Anne Marie, you're a pillar of strength and love, and an inspiration xxx

11/10/2017 Anne marie: My lovely friends, Marley has Sarcoma a rare type of Cancer and if it wasn't for the time we have been given to research, cross reference...We would be a mess right now in the throws of panic and hysteria...thanks to amazing survivors like Chris Wark and their coaching we feel informed and strong..It is in Marley's hands ..we have faith in the surgeons. Everyone of us is unique..there is no known case exactly like Marley so statistics mean nothing to us.

Marley is having a lovely time in Brighton with Archie. I just had to tell him over the phone as he asked about an oncologist appointment...he said "Mum I know I have Cancer but I want to stay in Brighton another night"

If you are interested..youtube chrisbeatcancer...1st things first.xxx

My new affirmation is "Marley is already healing"

Shirley: That's my new affirmation now as well .....

Jilly□: Darling brave Marley for staying on in Brighton. If anyone can fight this, with all the love he has behind him, he can. You hear about it all the time, defeating the odds - and the odds get better every day with the medical excellence we have now. 'Marley is already healing'. And we are on this journey with you all xxxxx

Luciana: Mantra is being said hourly, never mind daily! Love you all and please tell us if we can do anything at all xxxxx

Karen: Right here anytime .. feeling the love & peace alongside ... " let's fight the f*cker " ... Marley you are an inspiration to us all

Helen Mag: Much love to you all. Marley is strong like you and I know he will fight with every beat of his heart

Sharon: I watched the chrisbeatcancer vid. Very inspirational. Is this the healing route Marley has chosen? Marley is a hero, kind heart, fierce mind, brave spirit.

Catherine: Dearest Anne-Marie. All my love and thoughts to you and Andy and your lovely children. Re Chris Wark I will be diverting all Bertie's veggie garden produce to your doorstep xxxx

Anne marie: Thank you everyone ..love you all and appreciate these messages. I feel strong tonight and happy that the boys are having a nice time.

Gracie Angel: We just went for Mexican food and now the three of us are at Marleys watching TV and relaxing. Having the best time! Xxxxx

Anne Marie: ahh so nice to hear...so happy you are all together...a great comfort...love you Gracie girl

Gracie M: thats so nice to hear.. please give my two cousins a big cuddle from me, thanks gracie!! xxxxx

Gracie Angel: Bought Marley a head massager for his bday before he left as he said his head was hurting. Didn't get the chance to give it to him until now. He's eating chocolate and I'm massaging his head like a princess

Anne marie: We had a great meeting no upset at all because Marley was listened to after all the suggestions and protocol and Dr Wong agreed...surgery no Chemo no radio...the surgery is a huge risk in its self...but Marley is eating like a horse and stronger..He was articulate, calm and assertive and was in good humour. I felt so relieved that whatever happens to my boy he got to make the decisions which meant a lot to him. Dr Wong was happy and agreed after the crazy surgeons have done their job he will be happy to monitor Marley closely.so now new affirmation "The surgeons at the Brompton are amazingly gifted" will get a date next week

Clare Sis: Marley amazes me every day. The surgeons have cutting edge techniques there and no that's not my joke of the day x

Wonderful news. So glad they're being so supportive of Marley's choices x

Helen: Dr Wong sounds like he's got it right!!! What amazing strength you all have to deal with this....for Marley to handle it all so brilliantly is from all your positive energy!

Karen: Hurrah for Dr Wong and all his rightness in allowing Marley choices .. incredible doctors and surgeons at The Brompton xxx You beautiful boy Marley

Jilly☐: Great news, Marley is a strong young man who knows his own mind and as such stands the best chance of recovering from the operation, especially with such loving support from family, friends and amazing surgeons. I hope they give you a date asap.

Helen: Hi So great to hear Marley was listened to and doing things his way, it's so important for him to feel in control of his treatment. You have all been so amazingly strong. Xx

Jess: Just the right path. Fantastic news. Thinking of you all the time xxxxx

Anne Marie: Hello everyone...Taking Marley next wed 25th for meeting at The Brompton then hopefully if fit enough op next Thursday 26th..xxx

Anne marie: Hello everyone...some of you already know but Marley's op is now mon 30th. we are off to London tomorrow for pre op meeting.

He's Ok..not the best day as he has caught a cold...but he did eat a big lunch....xxxx

Anne marie: We are going just for the meeting...just praying he sleeps well and wakes up feeling better to travel.x

Anne marie: I think he is slightly better if not sooo bloody grumpy...!!

Anne marie: well my friends on waking Marley he was not happy and not well just a cold, he didn't want to spend 3 hours on a train...so I called the med sec to see, as we were coming down on Sunday for pre op, that we could leave the clinic visit...she was yet again, cold sharp and unreasonable...so I told Marley we have to go...big drama me in floods as I felt sorry for him...so I tried again, yet again same response even meaner....so I called back and tried to get hold of Pauline the lovely operator who had been so kind before, she was not on duty but her mate said "what's wrong? " I broke down in tears and told her she said "I'll sort this out, hang on a min"..next minute Miss Begum the surgeon gets on the line.."that's fine, no worries as long as Marley is 100% by Friday let him rest and eat" After telling her how much I

loved her I sat and cried with happiness for human kindness. Then Helen called me at that moment...So the lesson is learn every person's name and always befriend the operators...I will shower them with chocolate on Sunday.

Clare Sis: Oh Anne Marie now I'm crying. I'm so sorry Marley has a cold you will HAVE to be a Rottweiler about other people around him make sure no one visits who has a sniffle and ideally wash hands I had a hand gel I gave and no one minded they all understood especially when timing of surgery is so important. I'm so glad you could reach someone with a heart and make sure you introduce yourself to that cow when you can and tell her how her attitude made such a difficult time so much harder for you .

Anne marie: ..He is going to be 100% by Friday...

Anne marie: I spoke to different operator yesterday regarding money from the government...I had to tell him after 25 mins of questions to just acquire the form how efficient he was but perhaps instead of the first question being asked in a montone voice, devoid of compassion,

"Are you or your loved one going to die in the next 6 months?", he should say "The first question is a very difficult one and I'm so sorry to have to ask you this but is your loved one terminally ill? Is he expected to die within 6 months?" ...he apologised and said it was a script and was under revision. I said that maybe but he was a human after all and could maybe think of changing the script!!

It actually made Marley laugh out loud!!

Clare Sis: Just Internet stalked Miss begun she looks lovely and likes hats

Anne marie: hahaha already done it

Anne marie: I just opened beautiful flowers from Miranda Stonewig sent from Australia...(she used to live in Ickleton)

Gracie Angel: Sometimes Marley is a real grump but he loves you guys. Just spoke to him for a bit, hopefully his spirits will be raised. How lucky he is to have you AM xxxx

Helen Morrison: What a morning you have all had.........as you say, so good to remember names, I have to write them down as can't remember but whatever it takes and thank God you got a result of what's best for now. Sunshine is upon you all. Warmth, brightness and strength.

Catherine: Maaate, Anne Marie, so many ups and downs. All the medical people you have contact with so important .... When people are positive/helpful/pragmatic you are just so thankful. What a journey.

Anne Marie: thanks for offer I feel I'm bobbing about in the Bermuda Triangle at the moment.

Anne Marie: Well my loves we are back in our sanctuary flat in London...we are so lucky to have it. Lung function test tomorrow then meeting with my new best friend (she doesn't know it yet, but the whole of Ickleton has stalked her on line)Miss Begum.

Stay calm, positive and strong

Anne marie: Had reflexology today with the lovely Sheena(thank you Karen) It was wonderful. Still am shocked by pressure point made me involuntary cry...not in pain...just needed that release. Now I'm having a large Gin. Love you lot

Rosie: Thinking of you all today; will light a candle for Marley. Stay calm and focused sending all our love xx

Anne marie: what an amazingly efficient hospital...bloody marvelous all getting us through quickly with each test because they knew we were parked on Wapping high St!! Love them all

Clare Sis: Yes special hug for those weary shoulders xx

Where's Marley??

Anne Marie: like a cocoon under a blanket hiding from everything...in a haze of sleep deprivation depression and uncomfortable stomach so lets move on..x

Jilly☐: Dear Marley, he has so much to contend with. I'm sure once the operation is over he will start to feel more positive. How is his cold now? x

Anne marie: his cold has gone!!!

Emma: I'm in soho. My break is 445-630 if you need cuddles xxx

Anne Marie: And if anyone else is in London and want to visit at the Brompton or have coffee?

Anne Marie: when we are getting out of the taxi tomorrow it will feel like you are all getting out of it and coming in with us...a huge crowd of Big Love X

28/10/2017, 9:57 pm - Shirley Clark: God, he's handsome!!!!

Karen: Those eyes

Clare Sis: Doctor Marley Zhivigo sleep tight sweet dreams

Anne Marie: So Big Love he is there hopefully watching a video. He sent a text to say he was ok.

I want Miss Begum to have had a lovely day, wake up refreshed and ready to do an amazing job tomorrow To take out the cancer but with her fine skill ,leave everything else beautiful and undamaged. I pray my son be relaxed and at peace knowing he is in God's hands and that so many people are praying for him.

- Debbie: All will be well my amazing friend. We will be thinking of him all day. Xx

Susan: Will be thinking of you all tomorrow, Miss Begum will look after and do her best to fix your beautiful boy. Sending you love and prayers, love you Xx

Sheena: Have trust in the team and hope all goes well. Love to you all. Xx

29/10/2017, Catherine: My gorgeous lovely friend, I will be imagining miss begums hands working with confidence and skill (I have stalked her now too), and sending you all strength and love. You and your family are one in a million, all this love shows just that. May the force be with you, and please pass the big love on to Andy too. Missed you last week, can't wait to give you a big big hug soon. We love you xxx

Anne Marie: ok everyone pray harder...bloods being repeated as concerned about last Friday's...if good enough op at 11am...Marley just sent us out...I am feeling as you can imagine

Gracie M: sure he's absolutely surrounded by angels, im sure grandma will be placing them with him 24/7 !!

Anne Marie: I'm sitting in St Luke's Church

Becca: Praying and lots of positive vibes, BIG hugs Becca xxxxx

Shirley: Must be very peaceful there. Recharge, stay strong. x

Jess: I can't imagine Anne Marie. □

Anne Marie: I told him where I am and said I will wait here until he wants me...he sent back a nice text saying no worries see you soon...I feel calmer...Andy is walking round in the grounds probably looking at the stone work..bless him

God grant me the serenity

to accept the things I cannot change;

courage to change the things I can;

and wisdom to know the difference.

Julie: I have that prayer on my windowsill it's was grandmas and grandads I read that this morning. I have asked Paul to light our thinking candle in assembly at school today too. Love you all so much xxxx

Clare Sis: Oh Anne Marie I thought I had prayed as hard as I could but found extra and am begging him for the blood to be ok for op at the 11 and all the clinicians to be on tip top super fast efficiency.

Anne Marie: yer but I know you....short attention span when praying.!!..it must be working because I feel lighter and comforted and not a snotty mess any more.

Clare Sis: Lill Sis I promise I'm on my knees a snotty mess

Anne marie: well get up and blow your nose it's gonna be ok

Clare Sis: Shove off

Anne marie: haha more like it

Anne Marie: Andy just popped in with a poppy for me...and yes he has read all the history of the church.

Anne Marie: so spoken to registra...to keep Marley safe they are now awaiting urine sample testing...what will be will be....going for a long walk with Andy round Hyde park I think

Anne Marie: Marley just called the blood markers are worse so they are investigating the cause...he wants us to do nice things and see nice things... he is on face book .x

Anne Marie: he is obviously needing time alone

Clare Sis: Ok he's in the right place and if they need to help him with some transfusion they can do it what's another few hours and I'm sure like seeing you waiting and worrying no point rather have nice things to tell him show him

Catherine Ford: You are 2 minutes from me Anne Marie if you want coffee? And a squeeze? Xx

Shirley: Don't know what to say (that doesn't involve the F word).

Clare Sis: Marley's blood test is because he swallowed a new five pound note yesterday they are keeping him under observation but so far there has been no change

Shirley: Oh Clare - I love you.....

Anne Marie: Shirley you can swear...don't hide it inside...Shout!!! and clare ...classic!!

Shirley: FOR F*CK'S SAKE!!!!!!!!

Sheena: Emotional rollercoaster for you but the team looking after Marley know what's best for him. X

Anne Marie: walking up to Buckingham Palace

Susie: Have you got a fit bit? You must have done 100,000 steps tramping round

London!! You'll be an expert tour guide!! Has the operation been rescheduled?

Anne Marie: **so they are investigating still but giving him an iron infusion...may go ahead this week. May send us home....we will see...Marley amazing as usual and apologised for sending us away this morning....he is the most awesome guy I have ever met!! Thank you for all walking round London today with us it saved me from jumping in the Serpentine and embarrassing myself as It's not very deep**

Anne Marie: and I'm dead tired

30/10/2017, 9:01 pm - Luciana: The Ickleton vibes are so strong at the moment I'm sure they can be seen from space. We love you all - get some rest

27Anne Marie: I want to wrap him up in love tonight x

Susie: Above all, clothe yourselves with love, which binds us all together in perfect harmony.

Catherine: Oh gosh I bet you do Anne Marie, you want to protect your little boy. Sending all my love to you and Marley. I stopped my bike on the way home, sat down and had a good old star watch and thought of you all, was mighty beautiful, especially after the Victoria line! xxxxx as ever, big big love Sharon Cousin: Please send marley my love. I've been thinking of him all day. Hopefully tomorrow will be a better day. et some rest, you all need it, even though I know it's hard to sleep. Thinking of you all xxxxxx

Helen: What more can I say to you dear Ann-Marie.....what a shitty day of waiting for you all. Rest well and sending blankets of love and hugs to you all. Marley is one strong Man! God bless xx

Anne marie: Good morning....another day...It will all work out

ok this journey has more bumps than expected so need even more great people to it to save my finger tip.xx

Sharon:with you every step of the way

Anne marie: awaiting Iron infusion vitamin K injection.

he has eaten well...in good spirits which must be divine intervention considering what he has been through...I am form

filling by his bed...prob go home tomorrow...shhhh dont tell Annie or Archie surprise!

Anne marie: hello lovelies..Marley's whiteblood cell count has gone up more from 16 to 19.... they said it could be antibiotics need another day.... if improved tomorrow will be allowed home for weekend mon too soon for op ...penciled in for next thursday.

Please send positive vibes to get that infection down ...nothing grown on any of the samples...it's a mystery. he is calm...xx

Debbie: They will look after him. Hugs. Xx

Anne marie: There is 38 of you lovelies on here, then there is the family in NZ, friends on FB...congregations of different churches, loads of us surely all that love can heal this....xxx

Anne marie: helen you are funny...white blood cells going up is not good it shows they are gathering to fight infection...but at least you made us laugh..

Helen: Oh!!!!! ooops sorry! X

Anne marie: we walk alot...we use the stairs at the hospital instead of lift now and he is on level 5....! i breath slow .I cry when I need to, blow my nose and find the strength again though "Big Love " and knowing the truth that Marley is strong and can do this.

Anne marie: my sis Sarah says this..

Today is a perfect day. Miracle shall follow miracle and wonders will never cease x love u all.

Anne marie: Lovely sunny day...A new day with new possibilities

Catherine: What lovely pics, thanks for sharing. Anne Marie quite right, a beautiful day, thinking of you, right nearby in Trafalgar Square if you need anything at all. Love you and big love to Andy xxx

Helen: New day new beginning breathe in the positive thoughts breathe out the negative. Xx

Sue: Morning Annie, you are a warrior and everything you do will be victorious! You are surrounded by love and power and hope and positivity we are all sending more directly to Marley and all of you! xxxc

Becky: Sending you lots of love and healing rays from the strong south African sunshine from us in Cape Town cousin mandy: I've just had over 100 messages come through. I'm in now haha. Love all the messages and pictures. Loads of love from all of us here at Worthen Farm. Mandy xxxx

Anne marie: WHITEBLOOD CELL COUNT GONE DOWN....!!! Helen....that is good.

Anne marie: still high so keeping him in tonight but so good to have positive news

Anne marie: Our amazing friends have given us the flat ....so will take him there til the op...he can eat rest and watch the Thames

Sue: That's amazing news rest up and get better Marley xxx

frances: Yeah

Anne marie: Night Frances...Morning everyone. what a lovely pic...hoping when we visit we can bring him back to flat today.x

Clare Sis: Hello Australia lovely photo to start our day !!! Hugs Francis x

cousin Sandy: Good morning all you sunny people.

Me and Dan working in a sunny garden now and hoping Marley gets to feel the sun on him today too. Loads of love xxxx

Anne marie: ohh me tooooo !

Anne marie: Just walked into room ...My boy smiling ear to ear...just went off for a shower whistling!!

Miracle after miracle and wonders never cease!

Shirley: Ahh, that's lovely!!!   Give him a hug from us!!

Rosie: Glad Marley is feeling the love this morning

Clare Sis: Glad to hear that - no pain today??? maybe feeling a little better with the tlc and nutrition stuff working ? Send him my love xx

Becky: Wow I love miracles may they keep showering.

Sue: Oh Annie, that's just wonderful. 2 of us having been chanting for Marley today, Marley is in our prayers NMRK! Xxx cousin Sandy: How's Marley doing today ? X

Anne marie: not feeling great but he always improves as the day goes on...he felt good yesterday and wants to feel like that again.booked him a massage...may help.xx

Clare Sis: Dad had an accident in the car xx will of course tell him xx

cousin Sandy: Oh no life is very scary sometimes,love to everyone xxxx

04/11/2017, Anne marie: Dad's OK, what a lovely evening...All my kids and Gracie...a board game ,pizza and lots of laughs...just what the doctor ordered

Clare Sis: Sweet dreams I am sleeping peacefully tonight knowing you are all together x

Clare Sis: Good morning how wonderful to wake up all together and see the sun shine on old father Thames . Have a start to your sunday. Will miss you at church x

05/11/2017cousin Sandy: Have a lovely day today. Maybe you'll be able to see fireworks over London and the river tonight ?

Lots of love xxxx

Anne marie: It's so beautiful with the sun today..It's wonderful to all be here.x

frances Morning !! Sending loads of love and sunshine from oz

Rosie: Hi Anne Marie hope the day going well and Marley eating and feeling stronger. Sun is shining but it is cold in London Town; beautiful day for walk along the river. Sending positive vibes and hugs to you all xxx

Anne marie: Thankyou...we had a good day..we walked around soho had pancakes...xx

frances: Lol it's windy today

Doing a morning walk thinking and praying for you xxx

Sending all good vibes from bondi xx

Clare Sis: Goodnight from a chilly Tadpole hall keep warm and sprinkle of sleep fairy dust on your eyes

07/11/2017, 9:44 am - Clare Sis: This amazing prayer came in from my friends in America who heard it on Sunday and thought of you all I pray for my friend/family member who is in the hospital with a serious condition. Give them comfort and strength to endure what they are experiencing right now and to help the family deal with the stresses of being removed from home, their insurance paperwork and acceptance, their employers that they'd be understanding of the missing employee, or anything else that I can't think of that would help them all endure in this time of crisis for their friend/loved one. Please help the doctors and nurses know exactly what to do in each specific area and to find the proper diagnosis so that they can specifically treat the problem. If this means the laboratory staff, the radiologist, or any of the other staff associated with the care of my family member amen

07/11/2017, **Anne marie: hello...bloods tomorrow and if ok op will go ahead on thursday...calm and very quiet day..researching quietly while he rests.xx**

Rosie: Hoping you both have a restful night and wake refreshed and ready for the day ahead. Thinking of you both sending all the positivity and love.

Anne marie: thanks I need it...xx

Becky: Sleep and dream beautifully

Love from windy cape town x

cousin Sandy: Thanks for the update, thinking of Marley and you all and hope his bloods are good tomorrow.

I know its easier said than done but we hope you can have some head space to relax a little, you need to keep yourself well and strong too. Love you all xxxxxxx

Anne marie: I'm trying...I need to go for a stomp...will do that thursday during the op or i will go mad!!

sheena: After a week of lows and highs

Sending my love to the boy with blue eyes

Jilly☐: Everything crossed for the bloods tomorrow xxx☐

Rachel Cousin: Hoping and praying that Marley's blood tests come back ok for the op on Thursday.

Just found this 2003 article about diet and the role dairy plays in cancer. I know you have this in hand already, but it's an interesting and most of all a very hopeful read.

http://www.dailymail.co.uk/health/article-171377/A-change-diet-cured-cancer.html

cousin mandy: Good article Rachel. Then I got carried away reading about Barbie lol

Sue: Morning sweetheart, praying for great results today. I hope Marley is feeling ok? NMRK!! xxx

Rosie: Good morning to you all sending strong positive thoughts for the day ahead what time is the appointment? Xxx

Anne marie: going in for midday xx

cousin Sandy: Will be thinking of Marley xxxx

08/11/2017Anne marie: Mrs Parish is on her way!! which is a big deal before flying back to Dubai and I know she hates hospitals and is petrified of illness...especially Cancer...

Clare Sis: Oh my god it's the glamorous Calvary thank the lord for god sake put lipstick on

Anne marie: hahaha...of course!!

lisa: x

Clare Sis: She even had a LIPSTICK EMOJI god we have missed you Lisa even I'm putting on lipstick now and I'm in Birmingham!! Must have power as I just got upgraded to first class and given water and bounce bars!!!

08/11/2017, 3:02 pm - Shirley: Ah, lovely that you get to see each other!!!

Shirley: Yay!!!!!! LOVE that!

Luciana: Rocking that lippy girls!!

Anne marie: Can't tell you how lovely to see someone from "normal life"

Shirley: Oh sorry, I thought you just saw Lisa Parish.....!!!!! Nowt normal about any of us

Sue: Hi Annie, is Marley ok for the op tomorrow? Xxx

Anne marie: waiting now to hear

Clare Sis: Hello my sis all fingers crossed heart in mouth tummy in air just praying for positive progress right thing at the right time and I can come up tomorrow afternoon I'm not normal but can be with you from home xxx love

08/11/2017, 5:24 pm - Anne marie: **Operation 8 am tomorrow !!**

Sue: Yes!!!!!!!!!

Aisha: Shall be thinking of you all & sending all the best wishes in the world

Debbie: Fantastic news. Xx

Jilly☐: That's great to hear, the waiting will soon be over and the healing will begin xxx☐

cousin mandy: Fantastic. Well done Marley for being well enough xx

Jilly☐: We will all be with you in spirit at 8am tomorrow xxx☐

Luciana: Amazing news!!

cousin Sandy: So glad, loads and loads of love to Marley and you all xxxxxxxx

Catherine: Amazing news. This is so great, thank the Lordy. It seems one shouldn't be excited at the prospect of operations, but I am at this one! Around in London as normal all day long tomo and evening too xxx

Anne marie: well me and Andy will probably doing laps around the whole city!!

Catherine: Bet you will, I'll be standing at the Trafalgar Square pit stop with orange quarters and lucozade! Xx

Susan: Wonderful news that the waiting is over and Marley is one day closer to being well. Will be thinking of you all, shall say a little prayer for you on my run tomorrow xx

Karen: Ooh ... only just found the 8 am tomorrow ... hurrah to moving onwards and getting the " C word " outta here ... mucho love to you all .. big kiss for the brave warrior xx

Becky: What fantastic amazing news .Well done Marley and all who are sailing with him through these seas. Holding hands and hearts.

Love love love

We will be breathing deep at 8 tomorrow

Helen: What a relief to be moving forward at last.....will be thinking of you all tomorrow and sending so much love and hugs for you all xx

Sharon Cousin: Will be thinking of you all tomorrow morning xxxx cousin Mandy: This is the day for a good result. Lord hold Marley in your hands and you be the surgeon. Your angels surround Marley and let your peace that passes all understanding be in his heart and also in all of us.

Frances: Beautiful

Sue: Sending our love and prayers for Marley, 7:11 am - Katie From Mill: Thinking of you all today. Xxxx

Clare Sis: All love prayers. To Marley and strength endurance to you and andy

Anne marie: just spoke to him, he sounded calm as ever...we slept well and both feeling calm too. Xxx It's going to take 5 hours. thank you everyone for keeping me afloat on the Bemuda triangle these last months...

Susie: Love & prayers. We are with you xxxxxxxxxxxxx

Anne marie: And Clare you can't hold your breath for 5 hours ...breath in breath out!

Sue: We are beside you while you wait ☐xx

sheena :Will be a long day for you and you will be watching the clock and counting the hours. Do something nice, eat something nice and take deep breaths when you feel overwhelmed. Love to you all xx

Debbie: All will Be well. We'll be thinking of you and Marley all day. Xx

Rosie: We will be with you all in spirit sending all our love. All will be well. Biggest love to Marley xx

Catherine :Beautiful prayer from Mandy, my heart and thoughts with you today. Courage Marley. So much love from all of us xxx

Emma: Thinking of Marley and you and your whole family today. Love the Merrells and Lowndes families. We love you. X

Anne marie: All those weeks ago Marley refused all music then one day as he lay in the sun in our lovely garden I put this on and it relaxed us all

09/11/2017, 10:38amAnnemarie https://m.youtube.com/watch?v=m607NVm eqH8&itct=CBMQpDAYASlTCKfA_Pmls dcCFQ3YFgodcTYMgzlHcmVsYXRlZEjA 3Z_PzNm_-S8%3D

Karen: Great song ...

11:19 am - Anne marie: All of you know that singing is not in my skill set but if I could I would sing him this....he hasn't slept properly for months...he might hate it but I'm indulging myself...

https://m.youtube.com/watch?v=RxZSP1Dc 78Q&itct=CAgQpDAYCSITCOjNqYWvsd cCFRMSFgodGJQIbjIHcmVsYXRlZEjYpu q2xtW007MB

cousin Sandy: Lovely, sing loud. Half way now xxxx

Clare Sis: Taking Annabelle to breakfast xx

Gracie M: give Annabelle a kiss from me please. missing the family at this time. love you aunty Annie been thinking of you all morning at uni. xxxx so much love in this chat its amazing!

Sue: Oh it's so so beautiful ..xx

frances :That was beautiful Annmarie xx

I may fell asleep soon but sending love and I'm here always

Anne marie: Go to sleep my friend It will all be OK

Rosie: Just beautiful I can hear you singing Anne Marie xx

09/11/2017, 11:47 am - Anne marie: Andy has gone off to fix some stuff for Gene...he had to poor guy or he will go mad but I had a bath, listened to beautiful music and when he gets back we are going walking together.

Shirley: I love Montserrat Caballe - such a wonderful, wonderful voice. Sadly singing isn't in my skill set either - but we could whine this to Marley in stereo - I think he'd appreciate the gesture!!!! Halfway now

1:26 pm - Anne marie: Andy back with me now...just phoned hospital still in theatre

Clare Sis: Bless doctor Begum

Shirley: Not unusual for it to take a bit longer than they first think.

1:41 pm - Jilly☐: I'm sure they are being incredibly thorough and not rushing the final important steps, not long now xxx☐

Clare Sis: Sending strength and patience to you all for the ticking minutes. Think of it as the peace of Nan nans quiet sitting room and her cuckoo clock

Sue: Thinking of you all xx

2:47 pm - Anne marie: at St Lukes...there is a cafe here...looking out at Hospital over the road. he is still in theatre but doc just said he went down at 8.45 am.xx both calm and peaceful

09/11/2017, 4:28 pm - Anne marie: He is out and doing OK

Clare Sis: Oh my god I love them so much. She can have any hat she wants

Shirley: Heroes!!!!

Clare Sis: Please turn around and hug your husband for me Anne Marie he looks like I feel

Anne marie: It was very tough for the team but they did it..she has had a conversation with Marley already...they had to cut the nerve but she ' see there would be any difficulty because of that because of his malnourished state she is praying that there are no post op difficulties....

We are not out of the woods yet ..xxx

Luciana: That is very positive my lovely let's keep that positive vibe going and let the healing begin

Anne marie: can someone tell mum and dad

Anne marie: he lost a lot of blood so he is having more.

Gracie Angel: As soon as he's strong enough... give him a big cuddle from me

Debbie :Step 1 done. Keep strong. Big hugs to you all. Xxxx

Sheena: Well done to the surgical team for their skill and now he needs tlc from the nursing team. A huge relief for you. Take each day as it comes and hope Marley goes from strength to strength.

Anne marie: Today 9th Nov will now be named Begum day.

Clare Sis: Yes it will !!! Begum.. Ross Day. I'm praying for all the healing of nerves and blood and him being in good safe recovery tonight xxxx

Emma: God bless you all x

Sue: Begum Day it is! Oh darling I'm so glad it's been done and I pray for the best and most powerful healing process to begin!

My mum and dad Declan and Lara send their love. I will chant for Marley every day. X

Sue: Oh! just saw pic of Andi. Please also hug him from me xxx

Julie: Oh thank goodness it's done, I can image the whole of 'big love' clutching their phones waiting for news. So happy to see your lovely faces. Onwards and upwards big hugs from us all. Praying for strength and heeling for Marley xxx

Karen: Whoop to the awesomeness that is the team of surgeons and nurses and the amazing NHS .. sleep and heal Marley ... sleep and heal sending love and huge hugs to you all ...

cousin mandy: Phewee

becca: Phew thank goodness for that, well done Dr Ross and Miss Begum for looking after Marley. Lovely to see your smiles. Now for the healing process to begin...praying for sleep and healing for Marley. Hugs Becca xx

Anne marie: we have found "The builders Arms" down Britten street...having a gin...we can't see him yet...not til 6

Sarah Sis: Love u all so much x

Rosie Smith: Enjoy that G&T you deserve it sending all the love x

Lucy: What a relief for the operation to be over. Onwards and upwards. Love and strength to you all xxx

sheena: Hope that G&T is a double! X

Helen enjoy your G&T....lots of love to Marley when you see him. Bet you can't wait xx

Jilly☐: Wow you deserved that gin! Give darling boy all the love in this Big Love chat. I am sure he will be exhausted but he can rest and recover knowing step one is done. Well done Marley, amazing surgical team and wonder-parents!!! X☐

Emma: When you see Marley tell him there are about 100 middle aged women wanting to give him a big cuddle! Squeeeeezes from the Merrells fam. J sends love from Manc xxx

Shirley: And what Emma just said about the middle aged women - but not me of course....!!!

Anne marie: love you lot!!

Helen: What a fantabulous day. Let the healing and strengthening begin!

Debbie: Fabulous idea. Probably quite cathartic and good for you too!

Anne marie: We spoke to one guy all week Fissel, he had same op . he said when he came round he thought he was dead and thought "oh well it did'nt work out so well". We watched him gather strength every day, find his voice again after he lost it after surgery, get the use back in his arm and swallow again...The human body is magnificent...

Sharon Cousin: Massive hugs to you, been thinking of Marley all day at work, thinking positive thoughts. I'm coming into London tomorrow if you'd like to meet up, even if it's for a half an hour. Want to give you both a big hug xxxxx

cousin Sandy: Biggest smiles ever over here !!XX (and gins too !)

So so sooooo happy Marley got through the long surgery ok and well done to the hero Dr's and nurses.

Loads and loads of love and strength to Marley to feel better and get well very soon.

Anne marie: ok his first words (in his usual voice) were rude then he said "i need an ice lolly" ...no paralasis in arms and voice as normal...thank you God..he looks dreadful as expected with a million tubes.

Becky: How amazing life is!

Emma: This is the first bit of news about this situation that has made me smile.

Katherine: Fantastic news.....

Katie From Mill: Wonderful news. Lots of love to you all xxx

Debbie: I think he's looking pretty good all things considered! Good work Marley.

Karen: Wow ... He does look good like the enemy has left the building. go Marley ...

Jilly□: Give the man an ice lolly! He is a hero. I am making him gin ice lollies for when he's better x□

Clare Sis: Thumbs up right back at him

Sue: Well done Marley you are the bionic man. Sending love xxxx

Clare Sis: We will all be watching over him while he sleeps peacefully tumour free and the healing starts xx

Anne marie: back at flat...when we were looking for him we bumped into him outside the lifts and I was overcome with emotion so was Andy then this complete stranger a huge man gathered us both in his arms and said "be strong for him, he will be fine"...when we left later he was outside and hugged us both as if we had known him all our lives..he reassured us that our son will be fine.what a wonderful man...

cousin Sandy: Love and hugs nite nite and sleep well xxxx

Jilly☐: I want to hug that big hearted man for hugging you when I couldn't. Sleep well my lovelies xxx☐

Sarah Sis: He was an angel sent to comfort u xxx

Rosie: What a wonderful man, so glad someone was able to give you both the hugs we all want to give! Big love channelled through him. I hope you sleep well sending peace and love xx

Helen: Love that man!

7:52 am - Anne marie: I woke up to a text from Marley!! last night I wrote him everything that happened .he text "Thanks for the essay Mum, it took me half an hour to read it, all the letters are moving" I could'nt be happier

Rosie: wonderful news go Marley xx

Sue: Oh Annie that's just beautiful

Shirley: What a lovely way to wake up!!!! x

Susan: As Hansel would say that message from Marley was a gift of love

Clare Sis: Bless him man of few words but always the correct ones . Happy healing today xx

sheena: What a difference a day makes ....

cousin Sandy: So great to see Marley walking about already !

Well done him xx

and thanks so much for showing us, its made us very very happy xxxx

Rachel Cousin: Just brilliant to see Marley up already. What a fighter!! xxx

cousin mandy: Yes I'll show mum and dad. Something to look back at when he's running up a mountain or marathon xxx

Helen: Wow wow wow....go Marley

11/11/2017, 9:49 am - Sue Cruse: How is Marley today Annie? Xxx

Ann

: I couldn't believe he was up and about so soon, amazing, fighting spirit!

Anne marie: It was amazing to see

He has had lots of tubes removed and is doing exercises for his lungs.xx eating well

sheena: He is doing well on his road to recovery

Karen: Toot toot toot ...

cousin Sandy: Go Marley !!! Xxxx

- Karen: https://youtu.be/OuTuGS3hXtM

Never heard this before today

11/11/2017, 1:55 pm - Anne marie: He is however acting like a crack head..not that I know any...poor guy...very agitated and can't keep still...

Clare Sis: Oh dear remember mum after hip replacement drugs are good but have an affect what do the nurses say

Lucy: General anaesthetic can do all sorts of weird things to your concentration and reflexes and he would have had quite a lot for that length of operation. However, nurses will let you know x

Anne marie: thanks Lucy it's horrible to witness wish he could settle for half hour at least...

I sort of knew this day would be weird. The surgeon told us.

I am hiding in day room to breath and relax...as yes was getting twitchy

Susie: Perhaps he could take you for a virtual stroll through his favourite haunts in Brighton!

Anne marie: I will try....

Clare Sis: Try slapping him really hard tell him aunty Clare therapy to reboot his reflexes if it does not make him feel better might help you

Debbie: It's probably the pain relief. Is he on a lot of morphine type drugs? It will settle as they are able to wean down the opiates. Horrid to see though. I like Susie's idea of virtual walk through Brighton.

Anne marie: yes he is on a lot.

Clare Sis: Ask nurse angel to check his blood sugar ?

Anne marie: again get off google!!

Shirley: Lol Clare! AM you said the doctors said today would be an odd day. Did they say why? My guess, same as most replies here are that it's the drugs, particularly morphine or opioids- made me behave very oddly. Especially when I took them yesterday... Think you're right to just put a bit of space between both of you from time to time. We all need that

Shirley: Hahahaha!!!

Anne marie: Oh it's the drugs alright...

Shirley: That was hahahaha! To you telling Clare to get off google!!!

Anne marie: Dr Kilcommons my fav Doc has on his mug "please do not confuse your google search with my medical degree"

Clare Sis: The word kill in a doctors name does not inspire confidence

Clare Sis: But kill commoners?????

Debbie: I'm not on google. I came up with that all by myself actually!

Anne marie: not you Debbie because unlike Clare you are an actual Doc!!!

Debbie:

Clare Sis: Err I prefer you to address me as PROFESSOR Clare from now on.

Shirley: Thank goodness most of us in here are either very lovely or mad as a box of frogs□!!!   I am of course very much in the second category!!!!!

Debbie: I actually am at work too, and I've not had to look at google once yet today!

Anne marie: Well Debbie I appreciate you looking after your patients and checking in on Marley..xx

cousin Sandy: Hope Marley is a little calmer and able to get some rest this eve ? Xx

Anne marie: he is...a relief to him that his bladder is working x

Clare Sis: Very positive bless him all those wires and tubes . Say good nite sweet dreams restful healing sleep xx

Sue: Wishing Marley a restful sleep, xxx

cousin Sandy: Have a good sleep tonight Marley xx

Tina ballerina: Hi Anne Marie , I'm so please Marley is up and about after his surgery , even though he is restless , I guess that's normal , the drugs mess with your mind. I for one had a negative reaction to anaesthetic and morphine years ago, not only did I kick out both my parents from the hospital I also made the staff get the surgeon out of theatre to speak with me because I was certain she had performed the wrong surgery lol I completely lost my mind , then after a day or so I was back to my normal self. Anyway I thought I could share my story to at least make you guys laugh a little.

Onward and upward ! every day is new day that Marley will get stronger and stronger. Lots of love

Anne marie: Thanks Tina it helps to know different experiences and it makes me laugh to imagine my Greek friend demanding a surgeon out of theatre!!

We drove home..we are in the village..I just wanted to see everyone for a min to check on my Mum and Dad. Archie and Annie...feels weird!!!

Clare Sis: Oh my god I'm just fetching Annabelle see you when I drop her off cannot wait

Jilly☐: So good to think of you back in Ickleton - and so good to hear of Marleys progress. Hope he channels the surge of post op energy into healing, he must feel like a caged tiger with all those wires etc... but I'm sure it's the effect of the drugs and also the body's response to the removal of the tumour and the fact the body is now energising and repairing. Love you xxx☐☐

12/11/2017, Anne marie: So Marley just rang and said he was feeling much better today and that maybe it was the meds but yesterday he felt really weird!!! so happy to start my day with a good phonecall.

sheena: Blame the drugs. He was on a lot and no one knows how the body will react to such a cocktail like he must have had. X

becca: Such good news that he's feeling better I'll go with Sheena there, a cocktail of the following would do that; I looked up what happens with general anaesthetic and the following was likely given; 'General anesthesia is maintained by a combination of hypnotic agents, inhalational agents, opioids, muscle relaxants, sedatives, and cardiovascular drugs, along with ventilatory and thermoregulatory support.'

Clare Sis: Poor marley must be frightening he's been through so much . X

12/11/2017, 9:17 am - Emma Merrells: That's good news. I'm a mentalist on anaesthetic etc. I apparently start screaming but have no recollection! Glad he's feeling more positive xxxx

He's bound to feel a bit weird on and off for a while yet though, poor love. Give him loads of love from us.

See you later xxxx

Anne marie: ok I will get a train down to Marley then tube it to Hackney. xx

Anne marie: Back on the train now. lovely pitstop to surprise everyone for hugs and refuelling...Specially nice to see my Dad focus and realise it was me and give me such a big hugX

Sue Cruse: That's great Annie! Glad you went home for a while, so good for the soul. Love to you all, so happy to hear Marley feeling better today xxx

8:25 am - cousin Sandy: Good morning Anne marie and everyone. Lovely sun shine today, good for a walk ? xxxx

Anne marie: hahaha shall i come downstairs...?

Helen: Happy Monday....lovely sunny day....sending oodles of love to Marley from us all and especially my Mum who has been praying for him at her church. Thinking of you all. So great that he is making such amazing progress.

Clare Sis: Good morning everyone what a beautiful day! Been for a lovely walk and the birds are singing a positive start to the week. Have a lovely walk with Sandi and enjoy the morning. So glad marley is seeing beauty enough to capture it. Very good sign and a lovely photo! Might have to start a blog for patients views from my hospital bed??

Anne marie: Back to see my boy after another lovely pitstop with cousin Sandy...Thankyou for everything, the walk in park, delicious coffee at Jimmy's deli and meeting your friend .

13/11/2017, 2:55 pm - sheena mobile: Wow! Tube free!

Clare Sis: I can see the nurses already in love with our marvellous boy

Karen: Look what a ton of love can do ....

Epic Marley

Luciana: Amazing!

Catherine: This is so fantastic Anne Marie, Marley looks so much healthier than when I saw him just a few days okay. I can see a real difference. Someone is listening xxx

Anne marie: Wow Miss Begum just came round ...he is allowed home tomorrow!!!! so we will stay at flat til thursday...Andy better get that room finished!!

sheena: That's fantastic - within a week post op!

gracie mila: thats amazing news, put the BIGGEST smile on my face xx

lisa: That is just fantastic! Unbelievable!!!! Xx

- cousin Sandy: Crazzzy great news, love you's xxxxxxxxxxxxxx

Anne marie: I am very happy but slightly worried at the thought of him leaving hospital..

Debbie: He is doing really well. You'll have plenty of support and you can always phone them. Give me a yell if I can help with anything. X

Rachel Cousin: Amazing news and just wonderful how much better he looks just a few days on. Happy homecoming!! Xxx

Anne marie: Thanks Big love xxxx

Sharon Cousin: That's wonderful news Annemarie! Please give Marley a very gentle hug from me xxxxx

Debbie: Claire is right. You need to really nail down where you go if there are any issues. There is no proper thoracics at cambridge so you need to know who will deal with any problems. I'm sure oncology will help but they aren't the best people to deal with specific surgical issues because they aren't surgeons! I'm sure they have a plan as they do the surgery for people from all Over the country. You just need to make sure you are confident you know where to go for help. With that knowledge you will feel more safe with the discharge. Marley (and you) are doing brilliantly and it's onwards and upwards on this frosty morning. Xx

Anne marie: what can I get Miss Begum?? I was thinking a voucher from Peter Jones so she can buy a hat! Debbie Is that allowed?

There are thank you cards all over the wards but it just doesn't seem enough for saving Marley's life and giving him a chance.

Debbie: She won't be expecting anything. Honestly the nicest things I get are letters that say nice things. A lot of the staff work really hard and try their best and actually we get really very little positive feedback. A letter talking about your positive experience and gratitude is all you need. How lovely that you are thinking of this now when there is so much else to be thinking g about. You are awesome. Xx

Anne marie: Ok on it!! I was thinking "The key to Ickleton" Obviously when we get it gated in the near future with Clare sitting in a booth with a shotgun.

gracie: hahaha that made me laugh!

Karen: Even if it's some really beautiful bath oil to wallow in ... with your letter saying how incredible she is xx

14/11/2017Anne marie: Ok they are keeping Marley in as he does'nt feel that

pain is quite under control just yet..I'm glad they listened and agreed.xx

Clare Sis: thank goodness I'm glad . No point rushing and having a set back. I know they have to get you out soon and life must go on but if there was any way aim for Monday if possible so you have a whole week to settle and get it right with back up that might not be available saturday Sunday

- cousin Sandy: Yes, better to come out when he's feeling confident about himself and happy about after care. Love you's xxxx

Anne marie: Eating like a horse .xxxx

cousin Sandy: Great, good to hear.

Sue: Hope Marley is feeling better today xxx

Anne marie: morning...yes hope he is.he needs the drugs but they make him very tired.

Shirley : I need drugs.....

And after that last comment - morning Mrs! Hope you all have a lovely day. Miserable out there though, a day for wrapping up well.

Sue: Bless his heart, it's a major op his body is still healing, it will get better, he is in the best place xx

frances : Love it .. I need drugs xx bless

I hope and pray he is getting better xx

Clare Sis: Good morning everyone . I am relieved marley is still in hospital and will get rest and good care it's not even a week major surgery and best they control pain and he is tired of course so there will some more healing. we are always In The right place at the right time apart from me last night when a whole committee turned up for the meeting I thought was tonight! Talk about wing it!!!

- Anne marie: Oh dear Clare...did they frown apon you? there will be hell to pay..Ickleton Society will not be amused!!

cousin Sandy: Good morning. Its good hes tired cause he needs to sleep as much as poss. The more he sleeps the faster he'll heal xxxx

Catherine: If you all want to feel better about your organisational skills I'm on the train to London for the second time this morning after dropping my phone in a puddle and taking the only set of car keys to work with me. Dog walker luckily found phone .... I had get off train, get another one back, collect phone and return car keys. I have missed two meetings, am 3 hours late for work, Silas is late for Sarah, and Justin has missed his only meeting of the day. Hoping everyone is now feeling better about their own lives!!!! So fantastic that Marley is eating, nothing better to make you feel like someone is healing xxxx

Jilly□: hope your day improves lovely x□□

- frances: Totally ! hope your day gets better sending love to you Catherine. Much love for bondi

Anne marie: Catherine oh Catherine that's a bad one!! In my mind i have organised a shepherds pie for your tea a deep bubbly bath, a massage and a jug of Shirley's famous medicinal Cosmo...it cures every bad day

Anne marie: Have you silently cried in a cupboard yet?...In fact wait...i will meet you...Tell me time and place?

Jilly I think that could be the title of a book on motherhood. Have you silently cried in a cupboard?□□

Anne marie: I think we all have!!

Shirley: I'm just opening the doors.....   Took me a couple of mins cos I had to make a jug of Cosmo first - priorities dear girls, priorities....!

 Doesn't surprise me that you winged it Clare - I think you're fabulous in tricky circumstances!   Catherine - wow that really was the worst start to a day I've heard in a long time.....   Really hope it gets better!

Anne marie: I could come in disguise!! I actually look like a character from Dickens at the moment...Marley told me and Andy to go get some sleep the other day because we looked ugly!!! he was on many drugs but he had a point!!

 Catherine Ford: Okay I only want to see you once you sort out that pooh hair. Mate I did box dye the other day and bloody window cleaner turned up half way through .... my life ...

frances: You do make me laugh Anne Marie

 Anne marie: Well none of you really know my friend Frances from Sydney....I always said she should write a book...every chapter so far is mental...don't think anyone would believe any of it...!!

Debbie: OMG that has just made me spit my coffee over the key board!! Anne marie: I will put it down to Son in hospital madness!!

Susie: Brilliant! This Big Love chat never fails to make me smile!!

Susie: Catherine I hope your day improves...I'm cleaning baked beans off my ceiling and it's not even my children's fault!! It's amazing how far they can travel. At least no cashmere bath mats or diamond encrusted tiles were damaged in the process!!

15/11/2017, Anne marie: Ok Big Love...I have a new friend called Zoe an A and E nurse from Colchester..she has been here a month..endriometis caused plura in her lung..she has a family in Chelmsford and it's too far for them to travel. She needs the fluid to go down to 0 on the 2 machines she carries everywhere..it's 600!! her lung needs to inflate. she was just starting her own business, building a house.she said she never kept still or stopped working and she realised in her hardworking vision she had become a mean person so has spent today texting her husband, her colleagues, her sister to say sorry..

I told her miracle follows miracle and wonders never cease. She sent her mum home for reading the bible to her non stop for a week!! I said Big love is powerful..

cousin Sandy: Give her a message of love and hope from me too xx

Shirley: Oh wow.   Poor girl.   We never know what's round the corner- and I think that's probably just as well. I found Bruce round a corner......   You're right Annemarie Big Love is powerful, she'll get there. X

Karen: Hello from Great Chesterford ...

Jilly☐: She doesn't look or sound mean! I hope she recovers soon xxx☐ ☐

becca: Hope and positivity winging its way from here too

Clare Sis: For you Zoe and all of us

Susan: If Zoe's your friend she's our friend too. When she is feeling better, she must come visit the Big Love xx

Anne marie: From Zoe .Ann Marie this has given me focus and hope. Thank you.

Anne marie: from Zoe...shall I just add her to the group?

Shirley: Why not! The more the merrier!!!

15/11/2017, 8:18 pm - You added zoe

zoe: Thanks for the add Ann Marie and hello everyone

Susan s: Hey Zoe. Welcome to Big Love

Anne marie: Zoe there is no group like this one!! I don't know if all the old messages come through. If they do there maybe hundreds!!

Shirley: Hi Zoe!!!   Yep, there are def hundreds!   Sometimes just in a day!!!!

Rosie: Hey Zoe welcome to big love !

Gracie Angel: Zoe how lucky you are to have spent the day with Anne Marie - she is an angel and how lucky she was to have spent the day with you I hear

zoe: Thank you so much for the lovely welcome everyone and I definitely feel the love . Ann Marie came to me at the right time I was so lonely and really needed all the love and encouragement. God bless you all.

Jilly☐: Anne Marie has a knack of coming into your life just when you need her. It was the same with me. She is wise and generous and has raised most of the children in Ickleton the past twenty years! As you can probably tell, we her mucho X☐☐

Anne marie: Our lives have all crossed for some reason and so very glad they did...On days when the darkest sunglasses were not dark enough Big Love hugged me.

zoe: Thank you all very much.

cousin Sandy: Welcome to big love Zoe, happy times are ahead xxx

Susie: Hi Zoe Welcome! Anne-Marie is indeed an Angel. We miss her massively but she's always in the right place at the right time!!

Anne marie: ahh Susie at last those affirmations are becoming common place....

Luciana: Welcome Zoe, you lucky lady to be hanging out with Anne Marie! Hope you get well soon,Big Love is with you

Anne marie: All there is to say is he is drugged up and an eating machine...as in non stop!! he does his exercises then

sleeps..he has a lot of sleep and food to catch up on.xx

16/11/2017, 9:27 am - Anne marie: we are back in ickleton tomorrow

Clare Sis: is it put the bunting up get dancers drummers and trumpets Day???? Or a quiet homecoming for now

Anne marie: errr you know marley quiet homecoming prob.

Clare Sis: Morning darling niece Gracie can I get bunting dancers trumpets for your homecoming then

gracie: yes please!! big celebrations family together again. v excited to see you all

Clare Sis: Ok will be a subdued force of nature for marley sighhhhbut inside cirque de solei

- Anne marie: Aunty Joy if you are reading all this if you are up for it we would love to see you on saturday...i will make a comfy nest for you.xxx 16/11/2017, Clare Sis: joy hello from Ickleton. Maybe Marley gets his don't make a fuss from you! don't think you have been forgotten we all are sending love and prayers every day for you as well and I lit candles for you and Marley in church last week Annabelle always lights a candle for you but she was not there so I did it for her .Annabelle and I were talking about getting married and having children last week and she said she's going to name any daughter after you as you are one of her favourite people in the whole world

16/11/2017, 11:27 am - sheena mobile: Don't come home on a train - too many people coughing and spluttering. Last thing Marley needs is someone's germs.

Anne marie: It's ok getting a car ...a nice clean car xx

Anne marie: on our way out the doors of the brompton but did not want to leave you Zoe...everyone blast Zoe with big love messages she was having a down moment..xxx

sheena mobile: Safe journey home Marley and Anne Marie and love and best wishes for your recovery Zoe. Your turn out the hospital doors next.

Anne marie: We are just round the corner Zoe...I asked them all to come check on you and i always say "I am always in the right place at the right time" " I get stronger every day" "everything i need is always provided"

Clare Sis: Awwwe Zoe of course your down! Have a moment I always find a good big blub clears the way. I feel sorry for you being there suddenly with such a serious condition away from your family life being turned upside down. So give yourself some sorrow . It's time to then concentrate on doing all you can to make yourself well mind body spirit. Sounds like your mum could be like Anne Marie a really caring lady so get her some other reading material about health and ask her to join you on your journey. Then breathe in breathe out one day at a time . Give yourself a loving goal say going somewhere warm in February? That's mine! Reach out to your family and friends and get big love 2 off the ground but we will be thinking of you x

I posted a picture of the hospital accommodation we had to stay in!!!

sheena: OMG find somewhere better to stay!

Clare Sis: Annemarie won't answer her phone but I'm looking now for two adjoining rooms hotel but I don't know where she is

Jilly□: Or, pretend it's a geography field trip?! Or you are backpacking somewhere interesting? So long as you two are warm and dry and safe? Xxx□□

Clare Sis: Ok marley messaged they are out for dinner and he said it's not as bad as it looked they will go back there ! Annemarie that was a really sad arsed video and voice lol!! See you tomorrow x

sheena: Good they are out for dinner BUT not great to sleep in a stinky room. I'm thinking big germs!

zoe: Hey everyone thank you for your love . I cried so hard when I saw Ann Marie and Marley leave. I have been here since the 26th of September and my Faith was failing me. Just wanted to thank you for your love and Ann Marie I fell like I have known you for the rest of my life. Please continue to say a prayer for me and I am so touched by your love everyone. God bless you all.

Shirley: Hope you have a good night tonight Zoe. Sleep well.

sheena mobile: People in life are like radiators and some are like drains Zoe. Embrace the radiators who give warmth and love.

cousin Sandy: Keep going Zoe,

Look forward to getting well, good times and sunshine xx

Karen: Hey Zoe .. sending big love and kisses from us .. you are doing amazing and it's a gift to you both that you and Anne Marie met ... cos we will get to see you when you come to Ickleton message anytime on here ... we will all pick up and boost you through the tough times xxx

But bloody hell .. that room is crapolla .... although the sheets look clean !!! If you want to ship out tonight book anywhere .. we can sort .. not the ritz obvs !!

Susan: Jaysus, Annmarie that room looks worse that my own. Zoe, you're not alone, there's lots of love, positivity and craziness on this group for you whenever you need. Sleep well and your day to leave will come soon xx

becca: Great to hear Marley out of hospital That room doesn't look too great also happy to chip in if not too late and you want to move.

Zoe you can do it, Clare and the others are right give yourself a goal something to look forward to (you deserve it) you've been through so much and have definitely been blessed by the presence of Anne-Marie. I'm looking forward to hearing you've walked out those doors too and in the meantime we're here for You

Shirley: With you all the way Karen - although, Annemarie, you could just   at the Ritz.....!!!!!

16/11/2017, 9:35 pm - Anne marie: clare calm down crazy!! phone was out of charge...we went to pizza express...tired and going to sleep. its only one night....This is what 60 quid gets you in london...thank God for our lives

Anne marie: I had a large gin i can tell you!!!

Sweet dreams it will all be alright...zoe if you wake in the night say those affirmations and if you are worried press that buzzer!! x

frances: Wow good morning all

What a night !!!

Sweet dreams all xx

zoe: Night night everyone and I feel positive already. I will do Ann Marie. God bless you all

Sue: Na night Zoe xx

Clare Sis: Happy homecoming day step 3 frosty and white here

Sue Morning Zoe! Sending good morning glorious happy positive prayers and love from Ireland xxx

Francis

Slightly confused as to last nights stay.... what did I miss? One minute hospital and penthouse next....? Either way hope all is well Marley is going from strength to strength, I personally love food so keep eating Marley!! Annemarie and Andy I hope you are looking after yourselves and all my love to Zoe stay strong xxx bondi today is looking stormy

zoe: Good morning everyone, I had a lovely night thank you. all the best to Marley and Annmarie. Lots of love Zoe

- frances: Your in our heats Zoe!! be strong today

cousin mandy: Heats is good. Yes Zoe you're in our heats too keep smiling as it's a wonderful tonic for all ills xx

Anne marie: I slept well.!!..you see positive vibes and jilly it was like school trip accommodation and when you are young you don't care do you...marley still sleeping

17/11/2017, 4:41 pm - Anne marie: home now xxxx

mmmmm I love Cambridge!!

Anne marie: love you all so much...made me cry!!!

Karen: Happy Birthday Andy xxx

Anne marie: he won't see any of these messages he is on a mission to finish the garden room...xx he is painting as we speak.

Anne marie: he got the best pressie anyway his boy home!!

sheena mobile: What a dad! Happy Birthday and huge kudos to Andy!

17/11/2017, 10:23 pm - Karen Shiers: Nite Anne Marie

Nite Marley

Nite Zoe

Nite clare

Nite Sheena

Nite becca

Nite Anne

...... this could take a while

17/11/2017, 10:23 pm - Karen: Nite John Boy ...

Annemarie it really is nice to know you're back just down the road

Anne marie: Lovely bike ride and a message from Zoe to say she is fine but whatsapp went down , not suprised probably over loaded!! her numbers on her machine have gone down to 210..!!!

Marley doing ok..it's topsie turvey in the house...xx

Sharon : If any help is needed just ask. Mark will be free this afternoon x

Anne marie: bet Mark will be so glad you volunteered him!!

Karen: Fantastic news on Zoe ... please shout if you need anything for house .. xx

Anne marie: Think Andy has done all he can now awaiting windows for tiny conservatory now...x

but we have got to do shifting around of beds at some point...that will be a day of DIY SOS.xx

Karen: shout if you need more .

18/11/2017, 10:10 am - cousin Sandy: Great to hear that Marley is fine and the little house is nearly finished.

Looks like you had a lovely and well needed bike ride, great to get your head back in order.

18/11/2017, 6:34 pm - Anne marie: What a lovely afternoon seeing Aunty joy and the family...Marley didn't need Morphine today..amazing

Anne marie: No bones showing either just a sweet soft tummy!!

Clare Sis: That's just he most beautiful magical news

Jilly□: Great news Zoe down to zero and Marley off the morphine, keep up the healing and the resting there is much to look forward to and celebrate xxx□□

Keep eating Marley .. Have Hershey's for you xx

Anne marie: no sugar...cancer loves sugar xxxx but archie can have it

Anne marie: We just went for a walk to the mill...it was lovely He noticed how much we had missed the leaves and conkers falling, fireworks...He did really well walking quite fast and started his anti cancer diet today with gusto...really proud of him

Sue: That is so good to hear Annie.

sheena mobile: Aw lovely. I'm happy to do a home visit Reflexology treatment when Marley is ready. X

Anne marie: ahhh I'm sure he would love that...will help with the detox!!

Anne marie: If anyone knows a personal trainer that has lots of experience with post surgery....

Zoe:The air leak stayed on zero and I will be seeing the consultant tomorrow and hoping they make a decision to remove the three chest drains.

Becca: Great news Zoe it sounds like you may soon be walking out that door and back to your family xx

sheena: Great progress Zoe!

Anne marie: we are good...a little better each day. I am basically a feeding machine and he is an eating machine which is fabulous . getting into the swing of it all...It is full on but it will get easier...xx

zoe: FYI....I was seen by the Doctors and they are planning on taking the tubes out tomorrow

frances: Go Zoe!!! That's great news

Anne marie: Thats great Zoe...really wonderful. i would have replied sooner but i spend my life juicing and prepairing food !!!

Marley is doing well...It is not easy changing your lifestyle and whole diet but he is trying and eats what I give him..takes load of pills .we are still turning house upside down. It has needed it for a while....

While we were in London our neighbour Kathy of 23 years passed away from Leukemia. She actually died from a fatal fall but her treatment made her dizzy. she had had Chemo.

Susie: Love and prayers

Jilly☐: Sorry to hear of this, was Kathy your lovely neighbour? X☐☐

24/11/2017, 11:03 am - Anne marie: She was and she would come out most mornings and say 'who have you got today?" and say hello to all the kids...the kids would chat away to her through the hole in the fence and she loved talking to them.

Anne marie: when I first met kathy on the corner of Brookhampton st she told me she was moving to the new development at the stackyard...i was pregnant with marley and so happy to have got a house..she was so kind to me and made me feel that it was all going to be ok, having a baby and moving...what a comfort she has always been. i will miss her and when i see her again i will have time to hear her stories.

She lost a baby to cot death and she never got over it, his name was Gavin...she is with him now and her amazing husband Keith....keith was a caretaker at the Genome centre...he was also a wonderful person with such calming wisdom...when he died the house was literally filled with cards and love from most of the scientists on campus who would go and talk to Keith on their lunch breaks...

They used to run all the kids Christmas parties in Ickleton ..

Jilly□: I met her when I lived in ickleton, her face was familiar to me from childhood so we got chatting. She was often on her bike. Lovely lady, how nice to have her as a neighbour all those years xxx□□

Anne marie: Marley says he feels great..this week taking on more each day of taking care of himself..getting a haircut, walking and prepping his food, remembering his many supplements and other meds..To look at him now you would not think that 2 and a bit weeks ago he had a cancerous tumour. His room still waiting for windows but we have done a huge clear out now all the toys including Woody are in boxes in the loft...Which was very hard as a true believer of toys coming to life at night but then there are so many of them now i bet they have a great time...Felt sorry for Luke and Han Solo trapped in a box with Bratz dolls!!!

26/11/2017, 6:11 am - zoe: Good morning all and sorry for being quite. Was feeling under the weather.

Last week I was reviewed by the Doctors and they found a pocket of air in my right lower lob of my Lung. As a result I had to have a drain inserted under CT guided scan and it was one of the most painful procedures. This was done on Wednesday evening.

Since then I have been spiking temperatures. My husband had to come and stay with me from Friday and he wait until things have settled.

The Doctors are still not sure what's causing the temperatures.

They had suspected the PICC line (a PICC line is a long catheter they put in your vein to in order for the Doctors and nurses to be able to give you medication and different treatment types or for antibiotics).

My PICC line was removed on Friday and my temperature has been up again twice since the line was removed so clearly that was not the source of the problem.

They took some blood cultures samples and result in that is pending.

Two of the chest drains were taken out and I have two remaining.

They did an x-ray last night and apparently the air leak is still showing.

This morning I woke up at 4am with a temperature ☐ of 39.5. After meds and the treatment they gave me the temperature is now 36.4. Best wishes from Zoe

Sue: Zoe sweetheart, I will be praying hard that things improve fast. I can't imagine what you are going through but I feel that you are a fighter! I'm fighting with you from over the water in Ireland. It must be resolved! Please keep us posted when you can. Thinking of you and sending big cuddles xxx

Susan: Oh Zoe, thinking of you. I really hope that they find the cause soon and can get you back on the road to recovery. So pleased that your husband is there with you, so you're not alone and remember we are here too for you. Hoping today will be a better day xx

Anne marie: We are all with you..I am lighting a candle for you and will say prayers...you are not alone.

cousin mandy: sending love and healing to you Zoe. Speak those things that are not as though they are . It will manifest xxx

Anne marie: Imagine your lungs like the healthy text book picture ...I always thought like a lovely tree with strong and healthy branches reaching out. Breath in....Breath out

The most beautiful people we have known are those who have known defeat, known suffering, known struggle, known loss, and have found their way out of the depths. These persons have an appreciation, a sensitivity, and an understanding of life that fills them with compassion, gentleness, and a deep loving concern. Beautiful people do not just happen.

cousin mandy: Love that Anne Marie xx

Anne marie: Someone sent it to me on a bad day...It took me out of anger.

Karen: Ahh Zoe .. so sorry to hear it's been rough days .. sending love hugs and healing vibes to sort asap .. hope you can feel the sun on your face today

Karen: Marley sounds like he he doing a fantastic job .. I like the sound of all the toys partying together in the loft now !!

Clare Sis: Good morning Big Love its a sunny cold day so we can warm it up with the wonderful messages and connections to each other ! Zoe sending you a hug it's two step forwards one step back but retreating is different from surrendering so keep that inner strength get good nutrition a simple chicken broth home made or bought from a. Jewish deli is anti bacterial anti fungal . Helps the body from inside out and a little milk thistle helps the liver also get rid of toxins . That's from the doctor Clare school if medicine! Have a blessed Sunday x

cousin Sandy: Dear Zoe hoping that today is a good one for you and you start to feel a bit better again. Enjoy being with your husband, let love give you strength x

Catherine: Sending love and strength to you, Zoe xx

zoe: Good evening everyone, OMG!!! such uplifting and encouraging messages. I love you all and thank you. I am going to fight this.

Was not too well most of the day but I am looking forward to a brand new day tomorrow.

27/11/2017, 8:47 am - zoe: Good morning BIG Love

Today I woke up with a normal temperature thank God.

I have also been told that my inflammation makers are still too high because of the infection.

I seldom get sleepy and this is why I am always slow to answer your messages. I love you all and I feel like crying now.

Annmarie thank you for introducing me to Big Love such a loving group.

Always remember that your lovely messages truly uplift me.

May God almighty continue to bless each and everyone of you.

Group hug and kisses from me to you all.

Ps, Today I am scheduled to go and have the PICC line inserted and I am a little bit scared scared of needles (even though I have been a nurse for almost 16 years lol). I also have to do some exercises on the Bike and lot's of walking so wish me all the best.

cousin mandy: Morning Zoe you could try taking the high dose Allicin tablets called Allimed from Allicin International. It's the active ingredient in garlic and this company is the only one that has managed to stabilise it. It has even got tested results on curing MRSA. We've cleaned up horses with massive lung infections on it and you can take it alongside antibiotics. It would also help counter the bad effects of the antibiotics. They will also give you advice if you email them on dosages etc. Xx

Shirley: Dear Zoe, thinking of you today - I'm not keen on needles myself but to have to combine a PICC line AND exercising on a bike as well - that really is a miserable start to the week....! Keep your spirits up and we will all be wishing you well - it'll work !!!! Sx

zoe: Hi Mandy, that sounds interesting but will they allow it on the NHS and do you have any research I can send to one of the Doctors to look at?

cousin mandy: I have a book and leaflet. I could take pictures of some of the relevant pages for you or get a book sent to you?

zoe: Might just ask my husband to buy me some. Thanks

cousin mandy: You want Allimed from this company. It'll come the next day. Each tab is

450 as opposed to the 80 at Boots. You need to hit infections hard and take 6 a day. They may even say more.

Clare Sis: Wow Mandy that's amazing hope Anne Marie sees it can you slip some into dad's tea lol x

cousin mandy: Haha not easy to convince that generation

It has really helped my friend who had pneumonia and I had a bad bout of bronchitis I couldn't clear up and it did wonders. Also clears up fungal infections, detoxes body of viral cells as well as stubborn bacterial infections. But the dose is paramount to success. Xx

Clare Sis: That link gave me the link to Chris Walk which is what marley and Annemarie especially found incredibly helpful especially before treatment so a million thanks my wise cousin x

Rachel Cousin: Thyroid is a b*gger!! Clare, have sent email. So glad Marley is doing so well. Zoe - wishing you the quickest and best of healing. Good luck with the needles and all the exercising □Rachel x cousin mandy: We are like a health clinic chat line lol☐

Clare Sis: Lol BIG LOVE health happiness family caring it's a brilliant daily dose for me!

Sue: Marley looks amazing! Zoe you are getting out next darling onwards and upwards xx

27/11/2017, 1:46 pm - Clare Sis: Happy Monday to my wonderful nephew he is looking so much healthier but more importantly happy and that lovely smile coming back x

Anne marie: ahhh so happy It's not Christmas but it kinda feels like that feeling!!

Sue: That's the best Xmas present ever, joyous, xxx

I had the PICC line inserted but I am not going to lie it was painful.

Your encouraging words, prayers being made by family and my faith helped me to continue putting my arm down. We thank God.

I am still waiting for the Doctors to make a decision about the tubes.

Settling for an early night as in lots of pain.

Love Always

Zoe

Anne marie: get some oromorph!!

you don't need to be in pain Zoe

Sue: Oh Zoe please get them to help you darling

frances: Such love !!

Good morning big love!! Marley is looking wonderful!! Smiling and healthy !! Excellent xxx great Gracie is there as well □

Zoe sending all my love and hugs ..stay strong it's tuff I know but you will get thru this !! I'm not 100% sure what you have, But i can tell one thing....having tubes removed from your lungs is honestly the most painfully thing ever!!! I'm feeling your pain my love... I had two collapsed lungs and two fake lungs for a month or so... removing tubes was absolute hell!! If I could take your pain away I would in a heart beat xxx

Clare ....I have a thyroid problem as well... last year the doctors cut my right eye out remove a thyroid fat deposit and popped it back in... had to kinda cut all 4 muscles ... etc but I'm all ok now

Eyes are good

Lungs are good

Our bodies are amazing xx What's broken can be mended. What hurts can be healed. And no matter how dark it gets, the sun will rise again tomorrow

Rachel Cousin: The bravery in Big Love is just amazing. Salute!

Anne marie: Morning Everyone!! Night Frances. I told you Frances could write a book...!

Off to oncologist today that lovely Dr Wong, to see how we are gonna keep tabs.

cousin mandy: Yes I'm going to show them all cos they couldn't believe how well I said he looked x

Annemarie I know your oncologist is lovely but look on my Facebook at a video about someone challenging our cancer treatments in this country. Interesting.

Anne marie: I understand and I personally think the best sermon is through ones life for Marley to survive and thrive . Dr Wong is watching his back through this course of action...X

cousin mandy: I know

Anne marie: have seen loads of videos and documentaries...I look at everything

cousin mandy: I guess it does get to overload and if anyone tells me one more thing to look at I'll explode huh?

Your dad was singing your praises last night. How amazing you have been and are

frances: You have been amazing Annemarie!!!

zoe: I had Endometriosis which spread into my lungs and caused my right lung to collapse. As a result I had to come in and have the Endometriosis deposits removed and bare in mind these Doctors had never worked on a case like like this. It was truly God's guidance and I am forever grateful.

The problem now is that there is a bit of air in air some parts of the lung and the Doctors won't discharge me until the air is completely gone. This process apparently can take months.

zoe: Great testimony and really inspiring x

Rachel Cousin: Hi - you're so lucky with your consultant Anne Marie! Anyone with a good consultant is. And yes, you are amazing - much love to Marley and all.

It's so hit and miss with doctors. Some of you know this story but Dad's (prostate cancer) consultant has been arrogant, patronising and dismissive. She prescribed the maximum dose of a drug that at that level more than doubles the risk of sudden cardiac death in someone who has had a heart attack in the past (he has - and the leaflet in the packet warns about this), and it can kill through liver damage too at that dose - leaflet says your doctor might ask for regular liver function tests (she didn't) ... and Dad has just got over repeated bouts of sepsis due to blocked bile duct ... even the chemist said he'd never filled a prescription for that dose.

And that's apart from throwing him into the female menopause, with all the headaches/mood swings, growing breasts etc. Dad read the leaflet and point blank refused to take it - and it has to be his decision.

I asked the doctor if there was any alternative and she just snapped: "Well we could cut off his testicles."

She had never even done a scan, just blood tests. So we went to London for a second opinion and an MRI scan. £1,500 but worth it as we now know exactly what we're dealing with.

He's back on watchful waiting and new Doc says no need for such level of drugs, especially at 86. Horrid Doc - after complaint - now referring Dad to an oncologist - have met him before and he's lovely - kind, empathetic and extremely nice. Based at Addenbrookes, though we'll see him up here. Dad will be carefully monitored.

Apologies - this post has turned into a rant! Love and good morning to all. Mandy, will definitely look up your video. Zoe, Very much hope today is a better day.

frances: Your dad is lucky to have you Rachel ☐ hope new doctor is an angel !!

cousin mandy: This Big Love is amazing. I love all the news of everybody. It's a wonderful support network. Oh Rachel. You've been through a lot of crap. Your poor dad. Love you soooo much.

Rachel Cousin: Love you and think of the amazing things you have done Anne Marie. Miracles. xxx That's one of the most brilliant things about our family and friends and Big Love - all the laughing! Xxx

Sue: Hi Zoe, hope You are feeling better today sweetheart . Annie I love the photos and the anecdotes makes me smile xxx

zoe: Hello all, I have not feeling very well. I have been spiking temperatures since yesterday. They said I have an infection in my lung.

Best wishes

Rosie: Dear Zoe so sorry you still have this temperature what are they giving you to clear the infection ?

They have continued with antibiotic called Tazocin and today they have added Gentamicin. I really weak at the moment.

cousin mandy: It's like pneumonia I guess. Get on those high dose Allimed tabs. My friend improved greatly when he started them and he was on 2 types of strong antibiotics. Made him feel really ill. Also get probiotics for when you've finished antibiotics.

zoe: Mandy please can I get you to speak with my Mum. She wants to go get the meds you are recommending but is not sure was she is looking for. Is it ok if I give her your number?

Anne marie: Oh Zoe really sorry to see you have an infection...hopefully the antibiotics will knock it on the head...xxx

cousin mandy: Yes Zoe

Sue Cruse: Oh no! Zoe I'm sorry to hear that. I hope the meds clear up the infection fast, oh sweetheart stay positive and strong and feel will of all us ladies willing you to be better sending love and hugs xxxx

Anne marie: marley said he he could shrink down to molecular size he would go in and fight it for you

cousin mandy: Zoe go to www.allicin.co.uk and order product called Allimed. Take 6 a day. Can be taken at same time as antibiotics. Will help destroy infection. Or telephone 0345 2410505. They will give advice on dosages.

zoe: Ok thanks

Clare Sis: Zoe poor you also ty echenacia tea to help fight infections and milk thistle to support your liver neither of which interferes with other medicines also drink lots of elderflower cordial in water to flush toxins out in so sorry about the infection

30/11/2017, 8:04 am - cousin mandy: Morning all. Just listening to radio 4 on my way shopping yesterday and heard this. They did a survey on about 60000 people over 21 years and the ones who believed they exercised more than average even tho they didn't were in a bodily shape and health of someone who actually did. They couldn't explain it. Just saying how powerful is believing? Whether you believe for good or bad. So keep believing and knowing deep in your knower that health is already a done deal. Your cells will believe it if you do. You are all so courageous. Keep strong Marley and Zoe Xxxxxx

cousin Sandy: Zoe keep going. no pressure but we're all willing you to be better before Christmas ! Xx

cousin Sandy: Loads of love to Marley and Love to you Anne marie and everyone. keep warm !! Xx

30/11/2017, 12:42 pm - cousin mandy: I think that's why how you handle stuff is so important . I'm still learning x

30/11/2017, 12:50 pm - Rachel Cousin: Me too! Agree completely. Train doors just opened - no amount of thinking is going to make that warm air coming in! □so am going to embrace the cold- brrr!! X

Anne marie: Good evening Big Love...back at work this week which has been lovely to see the little ones. Marley had a good start to the week then over did it and stayed asleep for 2 days. But he was on great form today and managed 2 walks. Have to take each day as it comes...today was s good one!

Hope everybody is ok and keeping warm...or cool if in Australia!! Zoe thinking of you and hoping you have had a good day...or break it down further into hours...hope you could count a few good hours.

Karen: Nice update ... lots of love to you all x

zoe: Awwww hope Marley is ok Ann Marie. All the best back to work. I did not have a good day but hoping for a good one tomorrow. I am still here because of the infection and temperature spikes.

Night night everyone.

cousin mandy: Did you get them Allimed Zoe?

Anne marie: Sorry to hear that Zoe xxxI will pray tonight as always for you that your immune system kicks that infection...are you still on antibiotics? who is visiting you this weekend?

Jilly□: Zoe you poor love, tomorrow is another day, and a better one for you I hope. Hope they get that infection under control so you can heal and move forwards. I saw Marley today and it was so good to see his

beautiful smile and give him a (gentle!) hug
xxx☐☐☐

Sue: Na night dear Zoe, it must get better tomorrow xxx

Anne marie: "I breath with ease"

zoe: Hi Mandy she did and they will be coming today. Can't wait as the Doctors were starting to say that I was becoming resistant to most of the antibiotics.

cousin mandy: The older I live the more I see this is true . No matter our circumstances in life rich or poor the life experiences maybe different but they all go through the amazing, awful and mundane. It's what we do and how we live through each experience that causes us to grow in our characters. When we've felt pain we can feel for others when we've felt rejection we can include others when we've experienced poverty we can be givers . And knowing we're loved causes us to love. This Big Love is so full of love.

Zoe did your mum speak to them? What dosage did they tell her?

Zoe If that is the case with the antibiotics it's probably because you have developed a biofilm in your lungs which is a mucous type stuff that encases bacteria so antibiotics cannot penetrate. My advice would be to get a Probinano mini nebuliser from www.pruex.co.uk about £49 and some refills of the probiotic that goes in it. Easy to use. You inhale t as deep as you can and this breaks down the biofilm and you will cough up phlegm. Then order some Allimed liquid from same place you got tabs from and put some in the Probinano and inhale that straight onto your lungs. I have 2 probinanos one for each product. I'm still getting phlegm off my lungs after very bad bout of bronchitis infected bronchitis.. you can inhale as much as you like as it only does good. The Allimed tabs will also help stop the growth of endometriosis.

Gracie Angel: Loving these messages

cousin Sandy: Keep going Zoe, hope you have some times today xx

cousin Sandy: Hope Marley is doing well and everyone has a good weekend xx

Clare Sis: Incredible message today! Zoe big love reaching out to you ! Happy weekend everyone ! The lucky was with Shirley at Chesterford's charity night just as we were leaving they said oh we have found one more raffle prize ! Drew it and said SHIRLEY!!!

Clare Sis: Happy end to a great evening x

Shirley: I don't look in the least bit 'Cosmo'd'......!!!

i Mandy, I might have to chat with you separately. My husband brought the meds to the hospital yesterday.

Clare Sis: Hello everyone happy Sunday Zoe there was a prayer of the week in church today and I thought of you and lit a candle for you

03/12/2017, 4:03 pm - Shirley Clark: That's lovely Clare.   Hope you had a better day Zoe. X

zoe: Many thanks

I am staying strong just woken up.

Sue: Sending hugs xxx

zoe: Awwww thank you Sue xo

Sue: that's gonna be you soon xxx

cousin Sandy: Hoping Marley is doing well and Annemarie had a good monday with the children. Love to all the family xxxx.

Also good night to Zoe and we hope you had a better day today and sleep well tonight xxxx

Sue Cru

: Xxx good night all

Clare Sis: Good night everyone even John boy and half pint x

cousin mandy: Good morning

frances: Morning sunshine !!

zoe: Good afternoon everyone, as always thank you for sharing the love . I am making progress daily and yes I will soon be home too.

cousin Sandy: Great Zoe, keep it up xxxx

Jilly; Good to hear Zoe, hope you are getting fed lots of healing foods, keep up the good work

Karen: Whoop Zoe .. that's great news ...

zoe: Thank you all.

07/12/2017, 8:20 am - Anne marie: Good morning Big Love I slept well and can face the day better. Marley spiralled down last couple of days. could be because he came off the morphine..my heart heals quickly thank goodness because seeing him yesterday it broke but as usual the love and kindness of my friends and his friends and family have given me strength for the challenge of helping him battle not just Cancer but depression too which probably always go hand in hand....thinking of you all especially you Zoe and hoping everyone has a good day...stormy and windy here...maybe too much of a challenge for a bike ride!!

cousin mandy: We're with you Ann Marie. Love never fails.

Karen: Ahh darling .. he looked so well Monday but bound to happen .. will be massive roller coaster .. love you all and we're all here for anything

Jilly☐: Sorry to hear that Anne Marie, now he is clear of the morphine he can hopefully move forwards mentally too, is he open to talking therapy yet? I have two very good contacts in that field. Is he still doing acupuncture? xxx☐☐☐

Anne marie: yes booking accuncture and councilor today.xxx and getting him out in the wind...can you all will him to want to do that!!

cousin mandy: Haha even I don't want to do that. But I'm going out there now x

Clare Sis: Me too!! But I shall embrace it imagine I'm a huge. It's with a big wingspan and let it batter me across the meadows! Tell marley I'm planning to come and sit with him and have a good talk unless I hear he is making an effort to heal by walking that will get him running out the door

cousin mandy: Very funny Claire can't believe he would do that

Clare Sis: These youngsters have much more fragile complex feelings sometimes I'm not sure what to do to help and I'm not an expert in anything even though I'm Doctor Clare mode when I want them to feel better so I just be myself and hope that my example of getting on with it through ups and downs especially with humour might show them life's worth living and enjoying (and f*ck hormones!)

Clare Sis: Sorry whoops slipped out must be my hormones

cousin mandy: yes I guess as we get older some things don't seem to matter so much. Learn to laugh at ourselves but other things take over importance such as Marley and staying alive x

Anne marie: Dr Clare...the laughter specialist...yes Mandy that panic comes over me quite a bit then I have to kick it's arse...

cousin mandy: I know sometimes a little scream helps

Rachel Cousin: Hello - Anne-Marie, so sorry to hear Marley has been feeling rough. Just a quick check - I don't know if he has been on steroids but if he has and has come off them the withdrawal can tip people into a shockingly bad depression /Black hole. Solution is to go back on them via Doc and come off more gradually. No idea if this is what's happened, but just in case ☐ God bless. Love you. Rachel xxx

Helen :So sorry to hear Marley not doing so well....such a tough time and such a long road ahead to mentally keep positive. Sending lots of love and positivity.... 07/12/2017, 9:46 am - Rachel Cousin: Morning - hi Mandy and Clare and all. . All ok here thanks - how are you all? Is Uncle Robin feeling better?

Going to oncologist with Dad this afternoon for his prostate cancer (slow growing, fingers crossed). Pa is refusing - and we all agree - the chemical castration (maximum dose!) pills prescribed by snarky urologist - which he is contraindicated for anyway. (1) Has had heart attack in past so he is at risk of "sudden cardiac death" on these pills. (2) Leaflet also says "Do not take" if you have any other form of cancer - and he has a little kidney tumour which doctors are just watching. Apart from the side effects - female menopause, mood swings - and growing boobs!

Sue: Hi sweetheart, The lows after being on very strong painkillers for your back or similar is horrendous so morphine must be so much worse. You are a warrior! You are made of steel, your love and warmth will help him. Keep the doctors fully informed and get what you and Marley need from them. He needs to be around people even if he doesn't want to speak. Feel good movies, his favourites, his favourite music. Laughing. I know you are already on the case. You are a mummy from heaven. Warrior mummy, you will win! Praying and sending love and strength for dear Marley and you xxxxx cousin Sandy: We're willing Marley to feel less depressed, winter is such a crap time if youre feeling bad.

I hope you can persuade him to do something outside,

If not, cosy him up with love and try to get him into a project.

07/12/2017, 10:50 am - Anne marie: Do you mean involve the kids? They are very sweet with him and kids have a huge healing power because they don't judge..this week i got them washing the celery for him and they know to put their hands over their ears when he does all the blitzing. They think this is funny. He seems a lot brighter today. His friends have invited him to Ibiza ?..after they come back from a gig in Brazil!!! He was worried about no health care there but he is not sick as such and i think the winter sun and friends will do him a power of good.

: He just said "I will have a shower and go for a walk" best music to my ears. I think his friends are paying bless their hearts...or Air miles or something...anyway it won't cost a lot

07/12/2017, 12:20 pm - Anne marie: The walk is happening but just got coats on and the rain started hissing down..off in a min...humour...I had to laugh at myself yesterday...went out running clearing my mind from a bad nights sleep thinking of new positive affirmations."please let me stay physically fit to deal with this life". I tripped and stumbled big dramatic twisted starfish in road and hurt my ankle!! but that's life sometimes you ask for something and it gets worse but then better!!

07/12/2017, 9:28 pm - Anne marie: I'm so much better and so is Marley...he had a great acupuncture session after a great walk in the sun and lunch out and was happy that Adam the acupuncture guy was so surprised how quickly he was healing and looking so different from the last time he saw him...Marley's first night in the "Booth" tonight he said it's lovely and cosy...

Jess: Love to the booth and all who enter her

cousin mandy: Love you guys x night

Anne marie: Jess love love love Sam from crossfit so kind and so wonderful for Marley...gently does it!!

07/12/2017, 11:01 pm - zoe: Hey my Lovely Big Love Family. I have some fantastic news.

The doctors are going to let me go home for weekend leave. I will have to do my own antibiotics which is not a big deal considering I am a Nurse.

I really would like to thank you all for your support in prayers and love messages.

Annmarie and Mandy you rock. I was meant to cross paths with you too in life.

I will give you an update and send you some pics.

Night night Big Love

Anne marie: brilliant news

cousin mandy: Have a fabulouso weekend. So happy for you xx

Shirley: Zoe - that's absolutely fantastic! What marvellous news - just soooo exciting!!!!

Karen: How amazing ... enjoy your time out

zoe: I know hey! and I would have never done it without your support and may God truly bless you all.

I remember the day Annmarie left the hospital with Marley, I couldn't stop crying and Annmarie encouraged. Thank you.

Mandy if you hadn't introduced me to the Allimed products I would probably be still be hopeless and for that thank you.

It is still a journey but now I have hope.

Francis; Woke up to at least 60 messages today...

love to all big love

Clare Sis: Oh my goodness what a great end to the day!!!

cousin mandy: Morning all. It's a good day today. Claire you keep me laughing. Good for our souls

cousin Sandy: Zoe what great news ! Have a lovely weekend with loads of love, hugs and laughter xxx

Rachel Cousin: Hello - yes, have a lovely weekend Zoe - and all. Xxx Anne-Marie, hope foot/ankle is better.

Found this site - pic following. After oncologist told us yesterday that Lifestyle/food/sugar/eating veg makes no difference to cancer!!! They actually had a sweet trolley selling all kinds of sweets and cake and biscuits going round the cancer-dept waiting room ...

So - we're looking at this - among other things - baking soda to alkalise the body? Got to be better than a ton of Jelly Babies! Can't work link but this is the site ...

08/12/2017, 11:22 am - Clare Sis: Bloody hell what is this the dark ages are they suggesting leeches next! Of course food is your medicine and it's never to late to try! Cider vinger amazing for alkalising the body I took it in shot glasses with warm water till I got used to it and that was on the recommendation on a and e doctor when she saw me after I had the shoulder pain that almost finished me off calcinated tendonitis. Cured in 3 days I mean CURRED ! Health center said months therapy and nothing for Pain just tabs ! Thank goodness some enlightened ones out there

Sarah (howie): Processed sugar feeds cancer.....That's why cancer cells grown after certain scans because they use a special sugar solution to show up cancer cells. X cousin mandy: we could start our own health clinic. It does make me so mad because people listen to that crap

Rachel Cousin: Exactly! Thank you, Sarah. I don't understand why this consultant told us specifically that there was no proof that giving up sugar helped fight cancer ... or that eating veg would help ... x

Rachel Cousin: Mandy - yes!! So mad.

Clare - brilliant, three days - looked up the whole quote - I think we've lost something in our world in the past 2,000+ years - gained lots, but lost lots too, haven't we ...

It's tricky and unique as each person is or smoker drinker healthy eater bad genes pollution unhealthy sexual partners excercise or not so surely it's better to TRY than do nothing?? We are so so lucky with our health service but I hope one day Nutrition in hospitals will be a top priority for healing x

Oh yes and a top consultant now prescib s elderflower tea and milk thistle to help kidneys liver deal with chemo coming out of the body as he saw the blood data for a patient who did this and it was staggering he was private and the patient is alive and thriving

sheena: I'm all for natural and homeopathic remedies. I suffered from severe endometriosis for years had it lasered off and it grew again. Took homeopathic remedies and it went - Consultant laughed but did write down in my notes what I had taken to cure it.

cousin mandy: See. ...what wonderful information we all have and we're not even doctors haha

sheena mobile: Zoe would need to consult a Homeopath but the remedy I used was Sepia.

sheena mobile: http://natural-healing-guide.com/Homeopathy/Sepia.htm

zoe: Anything to help me as I have suffered for 18years.

sheena mobile: It's a little understood condition and other than taking the contraceptive pill continuously there isn't much else on offer. How old are you Zoe?

Sarah Smith (howie): Please do not take a remedy without seeing a homeopath. Different people need different remedies x they treat the person x what works for one may not work for another x back to my Christmas tree now x

zoe: Hi Sheena, I am 39 years old.

08/12/2017, 8:33 pm - zoe: Dear all,

Just been discharged for the weekend Home leave. I am a bit overwhelmed.

Jilly☐: Soak it all up Zoe, this has cheered my Friday night. Take good care xxx☐☐☐

cousin mandy: Norman from Allicin sends his Best wished to you and says keep taking the tablets xxx Have a lovely weekend xx

Zoe:Last night we arrived home late from the hospital and went bed very late also.

Right now I feel like a stranger in my own house. Norman (my husband) just finished giving the intravenous antibiotics and my pills gosh is was not easy. He has had to go to work and my mother will takeover from 08:30.

Sue: Oh Zoe am so pleased you are at home, sending big hugs xxxx

Jilly: Well done Norman, that can't be easy. And mum. Give them some Big Love from us x☐☐☐

Anne marie: Zoe it's gonna be weird for a bit .go with it, smile at your husband and eat some fresh lovely food...

Sue: Yes just allow yourself to be looked after xx

Jilly: How is Marley faring this weekend? I would like to buy him a massage or an acupuncture sesh, which do you think he would prefer? Or just cash for the Ibiza pot?! X☐☐☐

Anne marie: Thats so kind...x

12/12/2017, 6:34 am - frances kyrikos: Is everything ok Annmarie? Is marley going in for a check up???

Anne marie: morning frances.He is doing very well. we are going to see lovely Miss Begum to check out the surgery.

zoe: Hey Sandie, I was seen today and they are happy for me to go home tomorrow but will have to come in for Gentamicin blood level check every third day. This is a blood test they have to do as I am on an antibiotic called Gentamicin.

Helen: Good luck tomorrow for Marley, thinking of you lots. Happy days in Brighton.

Susan: Big day for the Big Love group! Thinking of you AM and Marley today, hope it all goes well. Zoe, so pleased you're able to go home, wonderful news. Take good care of yourself and enjoy every moment with your family. Good luck Frances, hope you hear that this wonderful new job is yours. Wishing you all a wonderful day

Susie: This morning as I prayed for you and Marley to face the day ahead an image popped into my head. I thought of the famous poem of 'Footprints in the sand' and God carrying you through difficult times, but instead of one set of footprints I could see hoards of footprints as everyone from 'Big Love' and beyond carried you all above their heads!!

Karen: Beautifully said

Shirley: Love that Susie.

Anne marie: Susie I love that and thats exactly how i felt on the dark days...xx

Jilly□: love that Susie

Julie: That's lovely Susie what a wonderful image x

Helen Love what Susie said....could not say any better. Hope you had a positive day and are doing OK. Thinking of you always xx

Sue: Great news Zoe! Am so pleased that you can go home. Annie darling so happy Marley is going to see his friends, that's what it's all about. Friends, family, love .. big love xxx

4:06 pm - zoe: All ready and just waiting for Hospital transport.

4:08 pm - Anne marie: maybe just maybe we will see each other...clinic 2 hours over

Anne marie: Zoe never mind will meet up soon...eat well, rest and keep in touch

Anne marie: keep warm everyone night night ❄

the meeting was good that lovely team greeted Marley with great affection and hugs like an old friend...he caused them a lot of sweat that day...they will never forget him. They were pleased with results and the fact he got off the pain killers so quickly.(maybe too quickly perhaps but he's off them). Sorry we did'nt meet Zoe but will soon.xx sheena mobile: Onwards and upwards lovely people

Clare Sis: Marley marley marley looking wonderfully relaxed

Karen: Fab photo xxx

14/12/2017, 1:19 pm - frances kyrikos: love to the moon and back dxx

Jilly☐: Gorgeous smile, thanks for sharing Grace x☐☐☐

Tina ballerina: It's so nice to see Marley smile! Sending all my love

cousin Sandy: Lovely photo, thanks Grace.

Its lovely to see Marley looking so much better a such a gorgeous smile too xxx

14/12/2017, 8:37 pm - Shirley Clark: Handsome boy!!!!

16/12/2017, 10:33 am - Gracie Angel: He wanted to do a thumbs up but it was too cold for him to take his hand out his pocket apparently

Anne marie: Hello! Really lovely evening listening to Annabelles choir in Cambridge....How are you getting on Zoe?

Rosie: Aww bless lovely to see what Andy has built for Marley. You are all amazing x

Anne marie: Can you see Marley in the window? if you come round he can tell you your fortune from the ticket booth

cousin mandy: When the rhythm of the heart becomes hectic,

Time takes on the strain until it breaks;

Then all the unattended stress falls in

On the mind like an endless, increasing weight.

The light in the mind becomes dim.

Things you could take in your stride before

Now become laborsome events of will.

Weariness invades your spirit.

Gravity begins falling inside you,

Dragging down every bone.

The tide you never valued has gone out.

And you are marooned on unsure ground.

Something within you has closed down;

And you cannot push yourself back to life.

You have been forced to enter empty time.

The desire that drove you has relinquished.

There is nothing else to do now but rest

And patiently learn to receive the self

You have forsaken in the race of days.

At first your thinking will darken

And sadness take over like listless weather.

The flow of unwept tears will frighten you.

You have traveled too fast over false ground;

Now your soul has come to take you back.

Take refuge in your senses, open up

To all the small miracles you rushed through.

Become inclined to watch the way of rain
When it falls slow and free.

Imitate the habit of twilight,
Taking time to open the well of color
That fostered the brightness of day.

Draw alongside the silence of stone
Until its calmness can claim you.
Be excessively gentle with yourself.

Stay clear of those vexed in spirit.
Learn to linger around someone of ease
Who feels they have all the time in the world.

Gradually, you will return to yourself,

Having learned a new respect for your heart

And the joy that dwells far within slow time.

~ John O'Donohue (1956 - 2008)

Sarah Sis: Mandy, that is an amazing piece, just beautiful. Hope u and yrs are well and happy. God bless you all and here's to a brilliant Christmas xx love to all my dear cousins and family and friends at this special time of year xxx

24/12/2017, 6:46 pm - Anne marie: Happy Christmas everyone...some of you may have got a card, some of you may not have but love you all very much!!

Karen: Love you all Happy Christmas Big Love xxxx

Helen Mo: Lots of love and wishing everyone a wonderful & Happy Christmas. Xx

Susan: This year has taught me it's not what you have in your life, but who. Happy Christmas Big Love xxx

24/12/2017, 11:21 pm - Shirley Clark: Happy Christmas all!!!

zoe: Merry Christmas Everyone lots of love from Zoe and family

Sue: Merry Xmas big love! Xxx

cousin Sandy: Happy Christmas every one, big love to all xxxx

Clare Sis: Been looking through my photos as I'm at the farm while dads poorly and have that precious time I keep talking about ! As the fire crackles it's a good time to reflect what amazing people have shared all the ups and downs of 2017.

Anne marie: Love you all Big Love

zoe: Good morning Annmarie. I miss chatting to you all.

zoe: Lung continues to be healthy

All antibiotics have been stopped and they will review me again in the 3rd of January

My mother sends her love to you all.

cousin mandy: Yay. Make sure you're taking the probiotics now xxx

Anne marie: That is so wonderful to read....absolutely wonderful!!

zoe: I am still on the Allimed pills and I use the Nebuliser too.

30/12/2017, 7:20 am - frances : Yep we are all here

How are you all??

Good to hear you are ok Zoe

30/12/2017, 7:20 am - cousin mandy: How's Marley Anne Marie? I missed so much news.

frances: Ditto !

zoe: Can't thank you both enough I love you and you were God sent and not to mention the love and support from this group

Will be starting those too and will keep you posted xo

30/12/2017, 7:24 am - Anne marie: Marley is doing so well. We are up early as we are going to Hot pod Yoga and we went to Crossfit yesterday...His new life is easier now and so lovely he says "yes" to most things suggested.. He has a trial at Stem and Glory next week a vegan restaurant...He is really pleased at your recovery Zoe

Anne marie: So proud of my broken muscles right now...could hardly get up stairs...loved it!!!

frances Love it Anne Marie and Marley!! Go team

Anne marie: We are moving like robots today...but thanks for the encouragement.

Karen: Before the rush .. Wishing everyone on Big Love lots of happiness , good health , strength and massive cuddles with your loved ones in 2018 ..

What an inspirational group you are xxxx

Aunty Joy: Love you all so much lovely see all and Marley looking so well

See you soon xx

Anne marie: Joy after everything you have been through, never heard you moan or grumble and you still have an amazing smile that lights up the room..

Aunty Joy: That's so nice xx

Joy by. Name joy by nature . Hello joy big hug from clare x

Aunty Joy: Hi Clare big hugs love aunty Joy xx

Shirley Clark: Hey Big Love. Been out of the loop for a few days - usual after Christmas colds, flu and bugs!!!! But feeling better now and when I looked there were 89 messages!!. You've gotta love Big Love!!!!

Hope you all had a fab Christmas and a very happy New Year to you all. So great that Marley is doing so well and wiping the floor with Andrew and Livvy, Annabelle just listened to your song - blown away - you really are fab! Zoe, can't tell you how lovely it is to see you, out for dinner looking gorgeous!

I look like a Muppet tonight so I won't be posting a photo - good job all the bugs haven't wiped out my shallowness!!!!!

09/01/2018, 8:59 am - Anne marie: Big Big love to Aunty Joy having her stint replaced today...we are with you my darling xxx

Clare Sis: Dear aunty joy thinking of the doctors and nurses taking great care of you today x

frances: We are all here for Aunty joy!!

Sending love and hugs from oz xxx

10:24 am - Aunty Joy: Still waiting xx

Anne marie: Marley in waiting room too xxxx thinking of you

09/01/2018, 4:14 pm - Sharon Cousin: Mum is all done and just waiting for meds to go home. The nurses and staff have been amazing xxx

Anne marie: Hello Big Love. just to pass on Marley went to oncologist the lovely Dr Wong today and they were visably moved to see him so well and healthy and going to crossfit!!. all blood tests came back normal...Iron, inflammation levels, white blood cell count, weight, all normal...have to be ever vigilant but we know when to celebrate a good day.xxx

Debbie: Amazing. I was wondering how he got on. Brilliant news. Xxx cousin mandy: OMG THANK YOU GOD UNIVERSE WHATEVER. XXX THATS truly fantastic news

Rachel Cousin: Wonderful news Anne Marie!!!xxx

Jilly□: Wonderful, wonderful news. Tears of joy. Keep up the good work Marley and warrior mum. HUGE love to you all xxx□□□□

sheena mobile: Thanks for sharing that good news x

Julie: Wow Annemarie that's wonderful news. I'm so happy for you all. Well done Marley, so much love to you. Thank you for letting us know xxx

Susan: It's a good, good day. Such wonderful news x

09/01/2018, 9:56 pm - cousin Sandy: Annemarie, such great news about Marley !

Well done to a great mum and a families love and care plus Marleys own mighty strength.

Love to all xxxx

What a great day!

Helen Mo: What amazing wonderful news following Marleys check up! He's done so amazingly well and will boost him to continue with all the effort you have all put in. Sending loads of love and positivity aways.

zoe: Great news I am so happy for Marley.

12/01/2018, 10:29 am - Anne marie: Im feeling very emotional

Clare Sis: So great look at that strength! H has found his determination from his gorg muma s fine example

18/01/2018, 8:30 am - Anne marie: Thinking of Aunty Joy and Sharon today...saying prayers for a speedy recovery for Joy in hospital and strength for Sharon...Xxxx

Clare Sis: Dear joy thinking of you today sending love and to Sharon xxx

Sarah Sis: Dearest Aunty Joy. We r all praying for you and send our big love to carry you and Sharon and the family through this time x much love

becca: Thinking of you and your family Sharon xx

Sharon Cousin: Thank you everyone, so kind of you xxxx

Anne marie: If the view from the window is a brick wall close your eyes and imagine us at the lake in france, warm sun and sunflowers everywhere

Shirley: Lots of love to Aunty Joy and Sharon. Xxxx

frances: Loads of love, hugs and get well soon to Aunty Joy

And thinking of you Sharon ... but I missed what's up? Either way Sharon I am sending you all my love from oz

21/01/2018, 9:44 pm - Sharon Cousin: Thank you Annamarie xxxx

Sarah Sis: Dear Sharon. Thinking of you and praying for god to give you strength and to give aunty joy healing and peace xx much love xx

Clare Sis: Hello Sharon it's not easy to bear when your mum or dad are unwell I am thinking of you tonight where ever you are xx

Sharon Cousin: Thank you everyone. So lovely to read your messages, I feel like I'm in a big hug xxxx

Sarah Sis: You are xx

25/01/2018, 9:29 pm - Anne marie: I had a good day today..I got 'outstanding' from OFSTED as some of you found out and it made me very happy and tonight I took marley to Crossfit, he asked to go and has been doing Yoga at home every day. Sam the coach was so lovely and When I promised him some payment soon he refused it and said it feels good to do something good for someone else...overwhelmed by kindnesses. and Annabelle really enjoyed football training tonight..really proud of my fitties.. It's good to celebrate the good stuff.

Aunty Joy, Sharon if you get to see this we are coming to see you!!!

we are bringing hugs, nail varnish, a juicer and veg!!

Susan: Oh Annmarie, congratulations on your Ofsted rating. However, that's no surprise to us, we've bloody known you've been outstanding since we met you. How kind of Sam, such a lovely generous thing to do. Sending you lots of love and best wishes to you and your courageous mum, Sharon xx

29/01/2018, 6:46 pm - **Anne marie: my love, Angels and prayers going out to Sharon keeping a vigil for her mum...Joy is too poorly to go home and the hospice is full so Sharon will be on a mattress next to her mum on a ward. I am hoping for a miracle and that a private room can be found .we love you Sharon and Angels will be with you all night...you are not alone. I got given a special candle today and will light it in your Mum's honour. Our love will be a warm blanket over you both tonight...we are here**

Jilly☐: Sharon May peace and love surround you at this difficult time. You and your wonderful mum are in our thoughts xxx☐☐☐☐

Karen: Am so sad to hear this .. sending love and prayers at a truly difficult time

Clare Sis: Dear Sharon the hospitals are full of Earth angels who won't let your mum suffer. I am praying for her peace and release and that you can be with her at the end. Tell the nurses to tell you the MINUTE they see the sighs that you may not so you can be holding her and telling her you love her. You are both in my prayers tonight xxx

cousin Sandy: We're so sorry and hope that your night will be filled with love and the knowing that family and friends are with you xx

Shirley: Dear Sharon, thinking of you and wishing you strength......

Sharon Cousin: Thank you all for your lovely kind thoughts. It means so much to me and my mum xxxxx

Clare Sis: Just thinking of you Sharon you will find some super strength to get through this but we are with you in thoughts and your dear mum x

Sarah Sis: Lots of love Sharon to you, yr Dad and especially yr Mum. Our prayers are for you to have peace and strength. Much love to you, you are a lovely daughter xx

30/01/2018, 8:19 am - **Anne marie: Godbless you Sharon ...Darling Joy passed away in the night..**

Clare Sis: Oh Sharon dear Sharon my deep condolences for your loss. Annemarie for you too I'm so sad for you all and send my love . Thank you god for taking joy peacefully and quickly at the end x

Susan: I'm so so sorry, I only had the pleasure of meeting Joy a few times and was struck by her positivity and strength. Sharon, Annmarie and Andy, I am thinking of you and sending you lots of love Xxx

frances: My thoughts heart and prays are for you Sharon and your family

Condolences xxx

Sending all my love

Helen: Our thoughts and prayers are with You All. So sorry for your loss. Helen x

Helen: I'm so sorry that your Mum has passed away, she was obviously a very special lady....sending love and hugs to you Sharon and all the family. Thinking of you all

- Sharon: Thinking of you all at this sad time and sending love. Sharon G x

Sharon Cousin: Thank you everyone for your kind words and your thoughts and prayers. My mum was truly amazing. She lived up to her name. Every where she went she bought joy and happiness to everyone.

She loved to make those she loved happy, every thing she did, she did with joy and love in her heart. She never complained and or gave in. She was determined right to the end that she would go when she was ready. She's gone to heaven to spread share her joy to others that we've loved and lost. I trying by best not to fall apart and your messages have been a tower of strength. Thank you. It comforts me to know just how much she was loved by everyone, and know she'd be deeply touched too xxxxx

Clare Sis:. She really was such an inspiration we have all been connected by andy and Annemarie to your family such a long time when I see that photo of you I remember you as a youngster so sweet xx

Sarah Sis: So sorry Sharon for yr loss. Yr Mum was a very special person and she shall be missed terribly. She is at peace now and we shall always remember her and the joy she made everyone feel around her. Love to yr Dad too xx

04/04/2018, 9:23 pm - **Anne marie: Well my darlings Marley goes for results of a CT scan tomorrow. He has a small blood clot on his lung left from the op. I will pray tonight that he is Cancer free. That**

Miss Begum took care of it and his Cancer journey will be a life changing memory..He is amazing, determined, calm and in good spirits. I too feel calm and I think I will sleep well.xxxxBless you all and Big Love to you all

Clare Sis: Good night to you all in my prayers every day always x

Susan: Sending you lots of love and positivity, I believe in Begum xx

Susie: That's a hug btw. I'd send one for Marley too but I think he's think I'm a bit weird!

xxx

Debbie: Love and thoughts coming from cornwall. Xxx

Emma: I pray the scan will go well Anne Marie. Thinking of you all. Lots of love x

zoe: Hello all and aww my prayers are with you Annemarie. We pray that all will be well with Marley and please send my regards.

I miss you all on Big Love.

frances: I pray everything is ok

Sending love and hugs xx

Karen: Having been in such a spiritual venue yesterday and waffted smoke all over for good health all will be good .. sending love , hugs and kisses from here to you all xxx

Jilly□: Sending you big hugs from across the pond, hope all goes smoothly tomorrow and the healing continues xxx□□□□

05/04/2018, 2:26 pm - **Anne marie: well my darlings we have been sitting in the sun thinking and talking....I will tell you in the same way he just told Gracie...It's not the best news as Dr Wong thinks the Cancer is present on the same site but it is not the worst news as there are things Marley still wants to try. I have had a secret cry and a swear and am calm like Marley now..It was always a possibility that it would come back but all is not lost...so enjoy the sunshine..we are.x**

Debbie: Oh what a disappointment for marley. Much love from us. Xx

Sharon Cousin: Sending a big big hug from me. Stay strong. There is hope xxxx

Clare Sis: F*ck f*ck f*ckity f*ck. I am so sorry. No doubt you have more info. Here for you all whatever comes next . Call me when you get back if you want a hug xx

Helen Ma: My heart has sunk at the news, but I know that Marley is strong and has a huge ring of support from friends and family that will be there for you all over the coming weeks.

frances: F*ck so sorry

But it will be ok xx stay strong

Sue: Annie I'm so sorry . We will all stand strong! We will fight this with you and pray for the best. Sending love

Helen: So devastated for you all....stay strong and amazing as you have been from the start. Lots of love and hugs to Marley xx

lisa: Nooooo! I am so so sorry.

But once again you are already facing this with such amazing positivity! Stay strong! Love to you all.

zoe: I am so sorry Annemarie. I won't stop praying for Marley.

Shirley: Well that's a f*cker Mrs.   Four square behind and beside you

Clare Sis: And this from Leisa who sends her love. She had major op and chemo for her cancer is a die hard scientist and had looked at every medicine all the combos every option since then and had to live with consequences she had not anticipated although she is alive....she said The really galling thing is we persist with chemotherapy to line the drug companies pockets whereas I feel sure there are answers out there if the scientists were able to pursue their own ideas and research........

06/04/2018, 12:35 pm - Anne marie: Thanks everyone...breathing welsh air, fed lambs and got my positive pants back on...all will be well. marley is doing yoga.

11/05/2018, 6:12 pm - **Anne marie: Haven't posted for ages! Marley did a gruelling 14 hour day yesterday...first day at work lifting freezers and heavy stuff for CDC(Thanks Simon)**

Karen: Go Marley ...

Sue: Respect!

Susan: Fantastic x

lisa: x

Helen: Oh my that sounds tough! X

cousin Sandy: Well done Marley, glad i wasnt moving fridges today ! Xx

Luciana: Fantastic Marley!!!! Xxx

Sharon Cousin: Awesome stuff Marley!!

Helen: To Marley! That's great news x

05/06/2018, 12:09 pm - **Anne marie: so My darlings I am standing in forest school with all the kids...marley went to the hospital for results of latest result...The blood clots have gone and there is no growth of the previous suspected recurrence. no spreading into blood or other organs...he has been so diligent so focussed so quietly determined...he is amazing. love you all**.

Emma: Wow. Amazing.

05/06/2018, 12:11 pm - Anne marie: a very happy day...btw the new vicar tapped me on the shoulder at that moment...in the middle of forest school....a special moment for sure

Sharon G: Wonderful news xx

Susan H: Oh Annmarie that is such wonderful news, so pleased for you all xxx

Debbie: Fabulous news. I'm so thrilled for you all. Happy hugs to you. Xxxx lisa: Bloody fantastic news! What strength he has shown! Xxx

Sue C: Yes!!! Yes!! The best news ever darling xxx

Catherine: WOW. So so so super fantastic!!!!!! Such the best news ever. So pleased for you all. Let's raise a glass/mug this PM!

05/06/2018, 12:22 pm - cousin mandy: I'm just crying right now. Total joy xxxx

12:23 pm - Clare Sis: Me toooo

12:23 pm - Sarah Sis: Miracle shall follow miracle XX so so happy

12:23 pm - Clare Sis: Thank god bless shat boy xxso proud of everything he has done and all you are doing and as a family

Karen: Woooahhhh ... that's super fantastic .... so much joy ... whoop whoop .. big love .. hugs and kisses

gracie: yay thats the best news. love you

Katie From Mill: Fantastic news! I'm so happy for you all. Big love xxx

Rachel Cousin: Such brilliant news!! Just brilliant!   Well done Marley Were the doctors thrilled too? Lots of love and to all. Xxx

Shirley: Thank f*ck!

Julie: Wow that's fantastic news, has made my day. So happy for you and your lovely family. Well done Marley you are amazing and of course so are you Annemarie. Love you xxxx

cousin Sandy: Brilliant, brilliant, beyond brilliant !!!

Love to Amazing Marley and you all xxxxxxxxxxxx

Aisha: Absolutely amazing news, I'm over the moon for you all. This calls for celebrations Big love

Luciana: AMAZING news!!!!!!

Sharon Cousin: That's wonderful news! xxxx

sheena: SO pleased to hear this

Helen Ma: Fabulous news! Marley has handled it all with such grace and quiet determination, just like his mum. Xxxxx

Hells bells: Amazing news!!

Becca: Wow that's amazing! The best news I've heard all year xx

Big Love continued to support me throughout his last month, his death, his funeral and those raw months that followed and are there waiting if I need them and while they wait they come up with some random, (mostly my sister Clare) crazy stuff that keeps me laughing while I go through this grief 'process'. I gave everyone on Big Love permission to leave the group but no one has, we are connected by love.

Stress relief

Notes, doodles, list of what or who you feel grateful for or perhaps to write frustrations or swear words down.

Notes

Notes

Notes

"May my footsteps stay printed on the long road less travelled, offering direction for those who come behind"

Jaoquim Osorio Martins Ferreira

Printed in Great Britain
by Amazon